Jeremiah

Jeremiah

JORGE PIXLEY

CHALICE
PRESS

ST. LOUIS, MISSOURI

Cover and interior design: Elizabeth Wright

This book is printed on acid-free, recycled paper.

Visit Chalice Press on the World Wide Web at
www.chalicepress.com

10 9 8 7 6 5 4 3 2 1   04 05 06 07 08 09

Library of Congress Cataloging–in–Publication Data

Pixley, Jorge V.
Jeremiah : Jorge Pixley.
   p. cm. —(Chalice Commentaries for Today)
Includes bibliographical references.
ISBN 0-8272-0527-9 (pbk. : alk. paper)
  1. Bible. O.T. Jeremiah—Commentaries. I. Title. II. Series
   BS1525.53P58 2004
   224'.2077—dc22

                                       2004005200

Printed in the United States of America

Contents

Series Preface

Chalice Commentaries for Today are designed to help pastors, seminary students, and educated laity who are open to contemporary scholarship claim the Bible in their personal lives and in their engagement with the crucial issues of our time. Although the various authors manifest a variety of interests and theological perspectives, they share a vision of God as a relational being, passionately involved in the life of the world, whose primary feature is love, and who both affects and is affected by the world. Their intention is to foster a dialogue between the world of the Bible and our own world and to do so in clear, nontechnical language with a minimum of references. The aim of the series as a whole is therefore a better understanding of the biblical challenges to the values, beliefs, and behavior in today's world as well as our own world's challenges to the values, beliefs, and behavior in the biblical world.

It is the conviction of the members of the editorial board of *Chalice Commentaries for Today* that the dialogue described here has had no better exemplar than the life and scholarship of William A. Beardslee, a founder of the series, whose original commentary on 1 Corinthians has provided the model for all the volumes to follow. It is therefore with great admiration, gratitude, and love that we dedicate this series as a whole to his memory.

Kathleen A. Farmer
David J. Lull
Russell Pregeant
Marti J. Steussy

Introduction

This book, a commentary on the biblical book of Jeremiah, seeks to read Jeremiah as a meaningful book for us today. Even when one approaches the Bible prayerfully, hoping to receive guidance from the Holy Spirit, one's reading, whether intended to be contemporary or strictly historical, will always be somewhat subjective, reflecting one's own perspective. So, I do not pretend that this is the only true reading of Jeremiah, but I do intend to offer the reader a legitimate and useful commentary on the text, a genuine "Commentary for Today," if not the only possible commentary for today.

The commentary in this volume is based upon the Hebrew Masoretic Text (MT),[1] with occasional reference to the ancient Greek translation known as the Septuagint (LXX), about which more will be said later in this introduction. Since there is no translation printed with the commentary, readers will have to read this commentary with an open Bible, which may be any of the modern translations. Occasionally, I will comment on the meaning of a word or phrase, but detailed discussion of issues in the Hebrew and Greek texts is not the main purpose of this commentary, which focuses instead on drawing connections between Jeremiah's world and our own.

This commentary speaks to a specific part of "today's" readership: It is directed at a Christian audience in the U.S.A. Should a Jewish man or woman or a Muslim one pick up the commentary, I hope that it will strike true also to them, but I am Christian and had a Christian audience in mind while composing this book. The other part of the expression, "in the U.S.A.," is more problematic. I was born in Chicago, of U.S. missionary parents, and grew up in Nicaragua. Although my experience is mostly in Latin America, I did do university studies in the United States and have frequently visited that country in my thirty-eight years of teaching in various Latin American countries. I lived over eight years in the United States during university studies and two of my three children now live in that country, as well as four grandchildren. But the United States is not my primary home. The reader must take that into account for what she or he thinks it is worth.

The Book of Jeremiah

Jeremiah is a prophetic book. It intends to gather up the preaching of a prophet who once delivered his poems or prose discourses in oral fashion. But it is itself a written book, written in the Hebrew language, which was the language of the prophet. Jeremiah was quite evidently a poet, and a good part of the book that bears his name is poetry. This is not just a matter of outward expression. A poet is a man or a woman who looks at life and society in a different manner from others and then uses striking language and metaphors that force others to think differently about themselves and their society. As school children learn, poetry is difficult. It is difficult because it recreates the language in a new way. Even more, it forces the reader or listener into a new way of looking at reality. This the poet often accomplishes through fresh metaphors. Since Jeremiah's language is for the most part poetic, we must expect it to be difficult—in Hebrew and in translation. But the book is not all poetry. It contains many prose sections, some of them discourses that purport to be Jeremiah's and some of them narratives about Jeremiah that try to give the reader a well-rounded image of the prophet. The reader of Jeremiah will find the prose sections easier to read than the poetic ones, but this is a normal effect: Prose tends to be easier to read than poetry in any language.

The book of Jeremiah, like other prophetic books of the Bible, has parts that express issues prior to the destruction of Jerusalem (586 B.C.E.[2]) and parts that reflect the experiences of the Judahite people after the destruction of their capital city. The prophet Jeremiah himself lived through that major crisis in national life and had activities pre-586 and others, fewer, post-586. But even the poetry from pre-586 and the narratives about events of that time have been written from both perspectives, so this issue becomes complicated (as it is with all prophetic books of the Bible). Judgment preaching dominated the period before the crisis of 586 B.C.E., which was assumed to be God's judgment, but after the crisis, when the people lived the trauma of dispersion in many lands, hopeful preaching seemed more appropriate. When the Persian king Cyrus entered the city of Babylon in 539 B.C.E., the whole situation changed again. Under the Persians, Judah became a province, Yehud, with limited autonomy. It became necessary to build for the future, both in the literal sense and in the sense of rebuilding culture and religion. The prophetic books were reworked in order to make them more useful in this major task of building up what had been destroyed. Summing up this paragraph, we can expect the book of Jeremiah to contain expressions of God's judgment before the destruction, often in poetry. But we can also expect to find expressions that come from the period after the destruction of 586 B.C.E., including some texts, usually prose, that narrate events prior to the destruction from the perspective of the events that came later. Finally, we can expect to find some editorial reworking that reflects the concerns of the rebuilding after Cyrus's entry into Babylon in 539 B.C.E. We will return to this when we turn to the text of Jeremiah.

The Structure of the Book of Jeremiah

Many interpreters feel that the book of Jeremiah is a hodgepodge with no notable structure at all. But it seems to this reader of Jeremiah that a minimal structure can be discerned and that this structure is in the shape of a ring around a center. Each section before the center has its corresponding counterpart after the center:

A. Prose Introduction (1:1–3)

  B. Prophet to the Nations (1:4–19)

    C. Judah's Sentence: Invasion from the North (2—6)

      D. Rejection of God's Word (7—10)

        E. Covenant Suspended: The Prophet's Impossible Role (11—20)

          F. Conflicts with Kings, Prophets, and Nonexiles (21—24)

            X. Sentences on Judah and the Nations (25)

          F'. Conflicts with Kings, Prophets, and Exiles (26—29)

        E'. A New Covenant and New Prophetic Role (30—33)

      D'. Rejection of God's Word and Prophet (34—38)

    C'. Invasion from the North Accomplished (39—45)

  B'. Prophecies to the Nations (46—51)

A'. Prose Conclusion: The Fall of Jerusalem (52)

The center of this structure is chapter 25, which speaks of the destruction of Jerusalem and a banquet where nations are made to drink the cup of God's wrath. What comes before is mostly poetry that is, generally speaking, from pre-586. What comes after chapter 25 is mostly but by no means entirely prose and presumably more heavily edited after 586. But following the doctoral dissertation of a Bolivian Adventist scholar, Jorge Torreblanca, I believe it is possible to discern a correspondence between what comes before chapter 25 with sections in what comes after it.[3]

In any ring structure, the center becomes the key interpretive piece. Already in chapter 1, we hear that Jeremiah is a prophet to the nations. The banquet scene in chapter 25 returns us forcefully to this theme. The last poetic chapters of the book (46—51) are a series of impressive oracles directed against all the nations within Judah's horizon, beginning with Egypt and ending with the longest poem of all, the one directed against Judah's nemesis, Babylon. Definitely, the book of Jeremiah is intended as an indictment of the nations, though no doubt the oracles themselves were addressed to a Judahite audience. The ring structure may or may not appear to the eye of the reader of this commentary who is also, I hope, reading along in the book of Jeremiah either in Hebrew or in a modern translation. Either way, let me propose that Jeremiah 25 is the topical center of the book and the key to interpreting the whole.

The Text of the Book of Jeremiah

This commentary works from the Hebrew Masoretic Text (MT), a text that was frozen by the sixth or seventh centuries C.E. and transmitted with amazing care by scribes and students known as the Masoretes. The scrolls discovered at Qumran, which come from between the second century B.C.E. and the first century C.E., show in many manuscripts a text that is very close to the MT. The modern English translations in use today were all made from the MT.

But another version of Jeremiah survives, based on an ancient translation into Greek. This translation was made in the third century B.C.E. in Egypt, where there was a large Jewish colony. In the book of Jeremiah, this Greek translation, called the Septuagint or LXX,[4] differs considerably from Jeremiah MT. It is considerably shorter, in part because it does not have some whole sections of MT and in part because shared sections diverge in many minor ways. Where the texts diverge, the LXX is almost always shorter than the MT.

Everything leads scholars to believe that LXX is the translation of a Hebrew original that did not look like the MT that we have today. Besides the relative shortness of LXX, there is a major structural difference. The poems against the nations (chaps. 46—51) come at the end of Jeremiah MT, but they come immediately before the important banquet scene (chap. 25 of Jeremiah MT) in LXX. When these six chapters are in the middle of the book, the ring structure of MT is shot to pieces. The LXX ends with a personal oracle to Baruch, which comes in chapter 45 in MT. The MT ends—if we set aside the prose historical chapter 52—with the command to Seraiah to throw the book into the river Euphrates as a symbol of Babylon's destruction. Interestingly, both versions of Jeremiah end with personal statements of the prophet to scribes who are sons of Neriah.

If we assume, as most students of the issue do, that LXX represents a variant Hebrew form of Jeremiah, the sixty-four thousand dollar question is, "Which represents the earlier form, Jeremiah MT or Jeremiah LXX?" Obviously, in a commentary such as this one, it is impossible to enter into detailed arguments for one or the other position, but it is my belief that the LXX represents a translation of an older form of the book than MT. Textual analysts usually assume that a shorter text is earlier and that a longer text includes expansions. I believe this is so in Jeremiah. When looking at the details, it becomes clear that MT has gone farther than LXX toward adapting Jeremiah to the requirements of nation-building in Judah after the return of many Judahite exiles from the various lands to which they were driven or in which they had taken refuge. Occasionally, I will mention these differences as the commentary progresses. Both surviving forms of Jeremiah come from well after the restoration in the late sixth century B.C.E., but MT should be seen as a later revision of Jeremiah than LXX. This later version has been reworked to give the book the ring structure that we can see in MT but not in LXX.

Imperialism in Jeremiah and Today

Many nations are mentioned in Jeremiah but the most important is, without doubt, Babylon. Babylon was the empire that ruled the known world in the days of Jeremiah and for several decades thereafter. After the demise of the Babylonian empire, the Persian empire arose and took its place in the world. This is outside of the direct horizon of the book of Jeremiah, although, as we have seen, the latest layer of editing may have been influenced by the rise of Persia. In the Bible, although there are other empires, the empire par excellence is the Babylonian, because it was responsible for the destruction of Jerusalem and the temple that was Israel's crowning glory. So much is this the case that in the New Testament book of the Revelation of John, Babylon becomes the cipher for the then-current Roman empire. This means that we too must read Babylon as a symbol of empire, in both our historical reading and in our application to the twenty-first century.

But what exactly is an empire? In the simplest terms, it is a state that has controlling military force. On the basis of its military might, this state subdues every other state within its horizon. Now, an empire may well have virtues that "justify" its domination of other states, such as the superior culture that the Greeks were proud to share as Alexander's mighty Greek armies conquered the known world as far as the Indus River. They (the Greeks) thought of themselves as a civilizing force that conquered barbarian tribes in order that the barbarians might enjoy the benefits of superior Greek culture. An empire may also have a religious tradition that it believes to be the only true one. The justification for Spanish "new world" conquests in the sixteenth century was the faith of Jesus Christ that the Spaniards brought to these nations. But Greek culture and Christian religion would have gotten neither one of these kingdoms anywhere had they not possessed superior military force and weapons (superior, that is, to those of the lesser nations of their day).

If we ask what state is the dominant empire in the twenty-first century, the answer can only be the U.S.A. The U.S. government controls an army with a military capability far surpassing any other on the planet today. And that military capacity stands ready to be used against any government that does or is perceived to do actions hostile to U.S. interests. To mention only recent events, it was used in Panama in 1989, in Iraq in 1991, and then in Sudan, Bosnia, Libya, Colombia, Afghanistan, and again in Iraq in 2003. The United States has, like most other empires before it, moral justifications for its use of force—in this case, the spread of democracy and the free market, universally recognized today as desirable. In the same way, Greek culture and Christian religion were generally perceived as desirable in the days of Greek and Spanish imperial domination. But democracy and free market are not freely accepted by all. When they are not accepted, they are imposed with overwhelming military might by the U.S. government. This is empire. This commentary will assume that when Jeremiah speaks about Babylon we can today apply much of what he says to the United States, with certain obvious differences. Empires have certain similarities in any epoch, and these allow us to read Jeremiah, a book about empire in the sixth century B.C.E., in our contemporary context.

PART A

Prose Introduction
(Jeremiah 1:1–3)

Jeremiah 1:1–3 and 52:1–34 provide a frame that places the sayings of the book in a general setting. These two passages tell the reader that this book is marked by the Babylonian exile, even though the reader will learn from Jeremiah 43 that the prophet himself was taken to and presumably died in Egypt. Two different contexts thus mark this book: first, the life, poetry, and times of Jeremiah the prophet; and second, the project and editorial work of scholars in the Babylonian exile community. This book belongs to both.

The exilic editors title the book "the words of Jeremiah" (1:1). Because, as we soon learn, Jeremiah is a prophet of the Holy One, the God of Israel, Jeremiah's words are also the words of the Holy One,[1] but the collectors of his work wish to draw the reader's attention to the person of the prophet. (The books of Amos and Isaiah have similar openings, while the other prophetic books tend to speak in terms of God's message rather than the prophet's.) It is an invitation to look at the man Jeremiah and the circumstances of his prophetic poetry.

The initial introduction of this man is done by situating his family origins—from the priests of Anathoth—and placing his life's work in relation to King Josiah (2 Kings 22:1—23:30) and two of Josiah's sons, Jehoiakim and Zedekiah (2 Kings 23:34—24:6 and 24:18—25:7). This excludes two kings among the last five kings of Judah, the ephemeral Jehoahaz (2 Kings 23:30–34) and Jehoiachin (2 Kings 24:6–15 and 25:27–30), who was very important to the Babylonian exile because he led that community from his cell and later from his house in Babylon. The ordering in Jeremiah draws our attention to Josiah, the first king in the list and the father of the other two. In the books of Kings, the "official" history of Israel composed among the Babylonian exiles, Josiah is praised as a good king who walked in the ways of David. This assessment was probably shared by the collectors of our book, who nevertheless allow us to know that Jeremiah did not share it (see Jer. 3:6–13). The other two kings are bad kings according to the official history, and, in these cases, Jeremiah the prophet agrees, as we shall see.

For our purposes, it is important to notice that, from the beginning, we are invited to distinguish the positions of the prophet from those of the Babylonian exiles who use his words in their project of founding a new nation of Judah under the umbrella of the Persian imperial authorities. This is a lesson in the use of a canonical book. We learn that we who recognize here an authoritative writing need to take into account the differences between the prophet and the word of God that he proclaimed to his circumstances and our use in our different situation of the word of God that we revere in the poetry of the prophet. The book of Jeremiah is about the pain of imperial domination and the consequent exile of the leaders of the people of Judah. Jeremiah 52:28–30 makes the surprising admission that the Babylonian exiles were a very small minority of the people of Judah. The exiled leaders, however, were the people who "counted" for the new Judean project of Persian times, and it is their representatives who did the editorial work on this book.

We in the United States must read the book of Jeremiah from our own setting. Jeremiah is a book about empire written from standpoint of the victims of imperial expansion. In today's world, the United States is the great imperial power. Many Christians in the United States identify with the project of creating a world subjected to U.S.-style democracy and capitalist free-market economy. A century ago, in the time of Presidents William McKinley and Theodore Roosevelt, with the painful experience of the "pacification" of the Philippines, the churches were more aware of U.S. empire than today. Today, we tend to take democracy and free-market economics as objective entities unrelated to the imperial policies of a nation that builds its foreign policy on a military force unequalled in today's world. In order to understand both Jeremiah the prophet and the book of Jeremiah, we must take some distance from current "common sense" and try to look at how the dynamics of empire apply alike to Babylonian, Persian, Roman, and U.S. empires. So we shall be looking at empire as we read Jeremiah through three different lenses: first, that of Jeremiah; second, that of the Babylonian exilic community; and, third, that of the Christian church inserted within the U.S. empire at the opening of the twenty-first century of the Common Era.

PART B

‒‒‒‒

Prophet to the Nations
(Jeremiah 1:4–19)

This unit of tradition contains two parts. In the first, Jeremiah recalls and bears witness to his calling by the Holy One to be a "prophet to the nations" (1:5–10). In the second, Jeremiah reports two visions that outline the content of his message as prophet to the nations (1:11–19). For the later compilers of the book, the prophet's role in the face of the nations is most important, since Babylon had destroyed the Judean kingdom and its capital city; Egypt, Moab, Ammon, and other countries had received refugees; and Persia had provided the space for a new Judah in the latter years of the sixth century B.C.E. This unit characterizes the ministry of Jeremiah and synthesizes his message.

The text we have before us is aware that the prophet's ministry is a destructive one, to uproot and destroy (1:10). It does not much matter to what extent the youth Jeremiah was aware of this at the moment of his vocation. The report of his calling purports to be given by Jeremiah himself but lacks any indication of the temporal distance from the event narrated. The word of God that a prophet delivers justifies his claim to be obeyed, and, for this reason, the call narratives were composed as credentials for a prophet's credibility. One supposes that the narrative was composed later to open the collection of Jeremiah's poems, when Jeremiah, his secretary, or even later scribes put his poetry into book form. As such, it is a mature reflection on a youthful experience.

The call narrative and the two visions that follow are very dramatic. The priest from Anathoth is to be God's spokesman to the nations, including the mighty empires of the day! The second vision, the one of the boiling pot, reveals that the purpose of the historical movement of the nations is to punish and then restore Judah. The Holy One, the God of Israel, moves mighty Babylon to assist in dealing with "his"—the Holy One's—apparently insignificant people![1] Though not named, the mighty invaders from the north were, in Israelite experience, Assyria, Babylon, and Persia. At the time of the final compilation of the book, Babylon, which destroyed Jerusalem and its temple, had become the archetype of mighty empire, the archenemy of Judah. Jeremiah himself lived through the emergence of Babylonian might, as Babylon dethroned Assyria and defeated Egypt before invading Judah and destroying Jerusalem. In looking back on his thirty-plus years of ministry, Jeremiah knew himself to be an instrument of the Holy One's sovereignty in using empire to punish the rebellion of the Holy One's people. The Holy One had made the prophet a fortified city, an iron pillar, a bronze wall (1:18).

The book of Jeremiah devotes many words to the rise and fall of empires, with Babylon at its center. In the horrifying scene of the banquet of the cup of the Holy One's wrath (Jer. 25:15–29) and in the collection of oracles against the nations in chapters 46—51, it is clear that this history only becomes capable of meaningful interpretation when it is read from the viewpoint of Israel, the object of God's sovereignty in the governance of world history. Jeremiah and his editors do not believe that the world moves according to the rules of geopolitical Realpolitik, as discussed by viziers in Babylon or professors at Harvard University. Instead, the book of Jeremiah claims, the sovereign God of the world has assigned Babylon the task of punishing Judah's apostasies (1:14–16) and given Babylon permission to subdue, in the course of its "mission," the other kingdoms of the world as well. This is a most remarkable reading of history and of empire! Surely, from the point of view of the Babylonian people, their king, and their army, it was a ridiculous misreading. But today, we, Christian believers set in the midst of the imperial power of our day, read not the Babylonian court annals but the book of Jeremiah as the word of God. Are we, like Esther in Persia, placed in an unlikely position in the midst of foreign empire in order to save God's people from destruction (see Esth. 4:14)?

In a world given over to Babylon by God, the prophet's mission is an unpopular one. He must stand up to the kings of his own country, calling on them to serve the empire and announcing their downfall if they refuse.

At the time of the siege against Jerusalem by the Babylonian army, he will call on the soldiers to lay down their arms and surrender to the enemy (Jer. 21:9–10), and he will be thrown in jail for doing so (Jer. 37:13–16). For his fidelity to the Holy One, the God of Israel, Jeremiah became a traitor to his nation at a grave moment of national crisis. It was a most unpleasant situation that would lead Jeremiah to cry out to God and against God on more than one occasion. Nevertheless, as the mature Jeremiah looks back on his calling, he feels that the Holy One warned him that being a prophet would make him an enemy of his own people, who would make war against him— useless war, because God was on his side to save him (1:19).

To be faithful to the God of the Bible can indeed be a very unpleasant matter. It will require at times a reading of history very different from what political science professors teach. Their reading of history necessarily deals with the acquisition and use of power. Jesus revealed a vision of history and social life in which he would meet his followers in the persons of poor people with desperate needs, precisely the least likely place to look for the heavenly Judge (Mt. 25:31–46). The Holy One is a strange God. When we think we have God near, God may well be far from us (Jer. 23:23). God's acts in history do not often appear to favor the poor, but, if Jeremiah is right, world history must be read from the perspective of the poor. This is highly destabilizing for Christian people whose lives are often lived very far from the poor and who have trouble imagining life as a struggle to survive day by day. Jeremiah read empire from the perspective of the God of Judah, even though the salvation of Judah, which was God's ultimate purpose, might first require Judah's subjugation to Babylon.

PART C

———

Judah's Sentence: Invasion from the North (*Jeremiah 2—6*)

———

This section is divided into two parts. The first (Jer. 2:1—4:4) speaks of the relationship between the Holy One and Judah as a problematic marriage. The second (Jer. 4:5—6:30) gathers together a variety of oracles intended to convince Jeremiah's hearers that all is not well and that doom lurks ahead if they do not repent and respond to the Holy One's calling.

The Holy One and Judah: A Marriage Gone Sour (Jeremiah 2:1—4:4)

This long and complex unit is made up of many poems and a prose section (3:6–18). There are several indications that it was put together by the *golah*, the community that returned from Babylon under the protection of Cyrus of Persia in 538 B.C.E. and other occasions later. The collection is dominated by marriage imagery and contains many parts put together in a rough manner not easy to understand. For easier handling, I shall divide it in two, 2:1–37 and 3:1—4:4, even though in the context of the book of Jeremiah it appears to be a single collection.

The marriage looks hopeless (Jeremiah 2:1–37). Like most marriages, the relationship between the Holy One and Israel began well with what seemed like true love, even though, in those early days, life was lived with great scarcity in the desert (2:1–3). In those days, anyone who failed to treat Israel respectfully was shamed and felt the weight of evil (2:3). As time went by, life became easier for this couple of lovers, since the Holy One was able to bring Israel into a land of plenty (2:7). Israel, like many married people, was not satisfied with comfort and soon forgot the benefits gained when the Holy One brought "her" out of Egypt and into a pleasant land (2:6). The prophets no longer taught loyalty to the Holy One but prophesied by Baal, an ancient god who gave rain to the peasants but also blessed the power arrangements of the kings of the land who respected no law to protect the needs of their own people (2:8). The wife Israel broke the bonds that joined her to her husband the Holy One and went after the gods of the lush land, prostituting herself under the green trees (2:20, 28). She went after rubbish and became garbage herself (*hevel,* which is often rendered "vanity" or "worthless" in English but can mean many things, including "foul vapor" or "rubbish," 2:5).

The image of marriage is filled out with other poetic images, the most striking one being the exchange of a fount of fresh flowing water for a stagnant cistern that has, besides, cracks so that it does not hold water (2:13). Similarly, a good planting of vines has been exchanged for one that is no good (2:21). In an image that tends toward pornography, the wife is compared with a camel in heat who seeks out any male that might come her way (2:24). In Jeremiah's application of the metaphor, the wife's lovers are sometimes other gods, as we have seen, but sometimes the mighty powers of Assyria and Egypt (2:18, 36). When the unfaithful wife is caught in the act of infidelity, she refuses to feel shame and even says wantonly that the wood is her father and that the stone bore her (2:26–27).

Poetry must be read and enjoyed. But when the poet is also a prophet, we must try to understand the historical meaning of the images used. We have been informed that Jeremiah is a prophet to the nations, but the nation that really matters to the Holy One and to the prophet is Israel, at times meaning the southern kingdom of Judah or its capital Jerusalem and at other times including the northern nation of Israel, whose capital was Samaria. The placing of this poetry about marriage at the head of the book makes God's concern for Israel absolutely clear. The book of Jeremiah is not a treatise of political or social history that tries to present an "objective" perspective on the nations of the time, large and small. These nations do indeed enter into the horizon of the prophet and the book, but neither the prophet nor the book's editors ever doubt that God's perspective is an Israelite perspective.

How are we, who are not Israelites, to take this scandalous particularity in our Holy Scriptures? As we understand it today, marriage is in its very essence particular and exclusive, as our Christian marriage ceremony makes quite clear when it asks the partners to renounce all others for the one partner present there to whom a solemn vow is made in the presence of many witnesses. The joyous intimacy of the two newlyweds cannot be shared with others without spoiling the relation, even though those others may be good friends of one or both of the partners. This initial exclusiveness seems to be required to make the relationship work. Hosea, Jeremiah, and Ezekiel all use marriage as a multifaceted metaphor for understanding the relationship between the Holy One and Israel (or Jerusalem). Jewish interpreters of the Song of Songs do so likewise. We who hold these books to be revelation from God can hardly discard this basic metaphor for the relation between God and the people Israel.

In keeping with Hosea and unlike Ezekiel, the prophet and book Jeremiah propose that, like most young marriages, this one had a wonderful beginning, even though its material circumstances were not very promising. In the ancient—and patriarchal—terms of Jeremiah's metaphor, the husband has full initiative in providing the goods required for the wife's life, beginning with the land that produces her food. The wife, as described by Jeremiah, has brought nothing into the marriage. She is not a rich merchant's daughter and has no splendid dowry. Since the young man, the prospective husband and lover, has found the woman in slavery and is buying her out, he can dictate his own terms: He does not have to negotiate with the bride's father. This would have been an unusual marriage even in Jeremiah's time, but it suits the fact that the nation to which he compares the bride is a small, weak one. Jeremiah does not "remember" the military might of David or the wealth of Solomon. The Israel of his prophecy is a poor and weak nation. The prophet to the nations, who in the course of the book is going to deal massively with Babylon, the imperial power of his time, does it all from the perspective of a poor and weak people, the nation Judah.

We must face the difficult theological issue posed by this metaphor. In Hosea, Jeremiah, and Ezekiel, this metaphor is a way of referring to the election of Israel by God as God's people, an essential pillar of biblical theology. Deuteronomy says, "Your God has chosen you out of all the people of the earth to be his people, his treasured possession" (Deut 7:6; the idea is also expressed in Deut. 14:2 and elsewhere). In Jeremiah, this belief is stated in the formula, "I will be their/your God and they/you will be my people" (Jer. 24:7; 31:33; 32:38, either in this or the reverse order people and then god). Without the election of Israel to be God's special people, the Bible makes no sense. Our Christian God is this same God of Israel!

What can this scandalous particularity mean for us today? To begin, in an historical view of reality where time and place matter, any revelation must take place sometime and somewhere, specifically. God, Creator of all, "chose" the planet Earth for the evolution of life, and not Mars or Jupiter. In like manner, God "chose" the human species for the most complex development of intelligence on this planet. Likewise, God "chose" Israel to explore and develop historical relations with a people. This "choice" brings both benefits and obligations, and it is as inexplicable as love (see Deut. 7:1–11). We Christians affirm that we are also heirs of this covenant between God and Israel.

We as Christians must preserve a special relation to the Jewish people, the other heirs of Israel today. Paul's image of the branch grafted onto the olive tree (Rom. 11:16–24) is an effort to deal with this. Paul believed that the original branches were ripped off to engraft the new ones. Later historical developments make it necessary to modify the image. The new branches, representing non-Jewish believing people, are engrafted alongside the Jewish people. In this manner, we can affirm the election of Israel while affirming also the legitimacy of the Christian inheritance growing out of biblical Israel.

But what can this metaphor mean in the realm of international relations today? Who, in the modern world, stands in a position comparable to the bride of whom Jeremiah speaks? One line of interpretation, going back to the earliest Christians, is to regard the Christian church gathered from many nations of the world as God's bride, the "true" Israel (Acts 28:23–29; Eph. 2:19–22). One may understand how Paul and Luke in the first century and Justin Martyr in the second could believe that in God's providence the Christian church would displace Israel. After twenty centuries of lively Jewish existence beside the church, it is less apparent that God ever intended for the Jewish faith to die out, while grievous Christian violence against Jews has given a hollow ring to Christian claims of moral superiority.

Others believe that the subject of Jeremiah's metaphor in today's world is the modern nation-state Israel. This does not seem appropriate, at least to this reader. The modern nation Israel has a mighty protector, the government of the U.S.A. Under the protection of this patron, it is able to carry out a foreign policy based on military defense. It is true that since modern Israel is surrounded by hostile nations, its young people must make a costly contribution to defend its survival. But in the larger geopolitical scene, Israel must be understood as an outrider of U.S. empire, its (the empire's) resident presence in the Middle East. As we read Jeremiah, we shall discover that the prophet believes that the Holy One uses empires to further the purposes of the special "marriage," and that for Judah's welfare her "husband" may even push her into temporary submission to Babylon.

But dare we assume that modern Israel's dependence on the United States is also God's plan? I find it repulsive to see God's marriage partner in a nation that depends on massive terrorism in Lebanon and Palestine and has supported terrorism in places like Chile and Guatemala. Such an interpretation will not help us build structures of peace that exclude states built on systematic violence and terror.

In our day, the people of the so-called Third World make up the vast majority of human habitation on planet Earth. Like Jeremiah's Judah, they are poor and have little defense against the depredations of empires. In reading Jeremiah from the U.S.A., we must make the mental effort to look at the world of nations from the perspective of the Third World. It will become clear in the course of our reading of this remarkable book that Jeremiah sees things not from the perspective of Judah's government but from the perspective of Judah's people, who may one day become the collective subject of a new political project. By the time of Jeremiah's editors, Judah has already taken on a new identity as the *golah* (the people who had returned from Babylonian exile). We would misunderstand if we compared the bride to the presently existing poor nations with their present governments. Jeremiah and the book that bears his name are thinking of a history of origins and a potential project for the future. Today in the Third World, states do not usually coincide with peoples of nations as they did for Jeremiah's Judah. The reader of Jeremiah may pick the people of his or her preference as the subject of the prophecy to the nations today. The reader might even think of a people that does not have a government, like the Kurds, the Miskitos, the Kikongos, the Aymaras, or the Kosovars. Or, she may prefer to imagine a generic Third-World people X or Y.

For modern readers, and probably for many in previous times, the very unequal relationship in Jeremiah's marriage metaphor is a problem. The marriage is presented from the perspective of a husband who feels wronged by his wife and does not recognize any guilt on his part for the failure of their marriage. Experience teaches us that in real marriages, neither party is entirely responsible when there is a breakup. In Jeremiah's poetry, by contrast, the husband is presented as entirely in the right, fully justified in blaming the wife for her unprovoked unfaithfulness. So, the metaphor's very portrayal of the dynamics of marital relationship is skewed and unrealistic.

The book of Jeremiah is also distinctly one-sided in its portrayal of Israel's particular history with the Holy One. According to the biblical confessions, Israel began life as a people whom the Holy One had delivered from slavery in Egypt. The overall perspective of the official history recorded in the books of Samuel and Kings puts the blame for problems in the covenant between the Holy One and Israel entirely on Israel's shoulders.

But that history also records actions of the Holy One that can surely be understood as provocative, if not downright disloyal to Israel. When we consider how the Holy One caused the ground to open up and to swallow Dathan, Abiram, and their families (Num. 16) or how fifty-thousand (or seventy) men were smitten at Beth Shemesh because they looked on the ark of the covenant (1 Sam. 6:19), we might wonder how the Holy One's own violence contributed to Israel's search for other lovers. We could also consider the Holy One's provoking David to do a census of the people and then punishing him and the people for carrying it out (2 Sam. 24), the outright partiality shown toward Solomon over his older brother Adonijah with no apparent justification except that the Holy One loved Solomon (2 Sam. 11 and 1 Kings 1—2), the divine messenger sent to deceive a king of Israel so he would go into battle to his own ruin (1 Kings 22), and many more stories taken from the official history. So, in addition to whatever problems we have with Jeremiah's understanding of marriage, there is also an issue of imbalance in his portrayal of history.

When all that is admitted, it remains true that in Jeremiah's view, Judah is at fault. The redactors of the book carry on this perspective with no critical doubts. So, our text tells us of a broken covenant for which Judah is responsible. This means clarity about the lack of innocence of any Third World people we may imagine as the wife God loves. It also calls for self-examination on the part of the church that today views itself as God's partner. Have we abandoned the God who took the flesh of a baby in a stable and who preached good news to *the poor*? If the poor are not at the center of our church's ministry, we are guilty of violating our covenant with God in Jesus Christ.

The Holy One proposes to restore the marriage with Israel (Jeremiah 3:1—4:4). The second section of the unit on the marriage of the Holy One with Israel/Judah runs from 3:1 to 4:4. It begins with a short poem that denies the legal grounds for remarriage (3:1–5) and ends with a longer poem in which the legal barriers are ignored and both marriage partners express the desire to restore the relationship (3:19—4:4). Sandwiched in the middle is a remarkable prose reflection that focuses on Judah in Josiah's time and after. The sandwich structure points toward the middle section, and the reader does well to begin interpretation there.

The prose section (3:6–18) complicates the marriage metaphor by dealing with two sisters whose identity is affirmed without poetic masks, Israel and Judah. Both sisters are rebellious and have betrayed their covenant with the Holy One. The marriage metaphor is in the background, especially in the mention of Israel's divorce in verse 8, but the focus is on the apostasy of both Israel and Judah, which is seen more as treachery and whoredom than adultery/divorce. The conclusion of this reflection comes in verse 11 where the Holy One declares that Israel the apostate is more just than Judah the traitor.

The basis for this judgment is not left to the creativity of the reader but is quite on the surface. On the one hand, the prose section is dated in the reign of Josiah, the reformist king who is highly praised in 2 Kings 23:24–25 and many other "Deuteronomistic" texts.[1] Jeremiah 3:10 is a clear allusion to Josiah's famous reform: Whereas apostate Israel never pretended to return from her sins, Judah pretended to return but it was a false return (here the word *sheqer,* "falsehood," is used, a favorite expression in Jeremiah's book). Why does this passage make this very negative judgment on a reform generally praised in the Bible? The answer must be sought in Jeremiah's (and his editors') nose for falsehood, what we today would call ideology. Josiah led a great liturgical renewal, which included purging the Jerusalem temple of images of other gods, but little is said about any official efforts to wipe out corruption or the exploitation of the poor. In the light of the "Temple Sermon" that is coming up in Jeremiah 7, we are surely justified in seeing this as the key to this passage. Religious renewal without justice is false, worse than no renewal at all.

Now, we can look at the poetry in Jeremiah 3:1–5, where the poet affirms the legal impossibility of a husband who has dispatched his wife reclaiming her later, if she has married another, even should that second husband have died. Such a remarriage would "pollute the land." This law can be found in Deuteronomy 24:1–4. Note the cross from "wife" to "land," a connection made already in the law. The law quite explicitly forbids a reunion. And yet, a repentant Judah wishes to return (Jer. 3:24–25), and a severe but affirming Holy One invites a full repentance and return (Jer. 4:3–4). Requirements for life and love can and must cancel legal stipulations. The Holy One will heal his faithless children (Jer. 3:22), a powerful and not-so-frequent metaphor of the divine physician. In Pauline terms, this is a case of grace rendering the law inoperative.

All of this leads into a reflection on today's "laws," the strongest being those of the free market, free trade, and free movement of money across national borders. Governments are today forced to submit to the laws of the market, the violation of which is considered a grave offence. But when, in keeping these laws, debt repayment causes inhumane poverty and even the deaths of millions of humans, surely justice requires suspending the law that requires debtors to repay their loans. When "free" trade destroys the livelihood of millions of peasants by flooding their countries with cheap corn, wheat, and rice, surely some trade controls that restrict the so-called laws of free trade are justified. It is a big subject and a very necessary one in today's globalized economy, which is designed to increase the fortunes of those who already have much more than they need or can spend. Paul, the apostle to the nations, gave Christians a systematic reflection on the fatal consequences of taking the law, even God's holy law, as an inflexible guide. But the idea is already here in Jeremiah 3:1—4:4.

A Society Menaced with Impending Ruin
(Jeremiah 4:5—6:30)

This long section has only one theme: In spite of apparent peace, Judah lives in imminent danger. The section is an anthology of poems that appear to come from an early period in the prophet Jeremiah's literary activity—a phrase intended to include oral as well as written composition, and probably more of the former than the latter. The Babylonian empire is nowhere named, suggesting that this is from a time before that empire was an obvious presence.

Also, however, Jeremiah does not seem to believe that the specifics of international politics are important for the question at hand, the imminent destruction of Judah. This destruction is inherent in the evils of Judah's social life, as some of the poems emphasize. The fundamental cause of the coming calamity is the Holy One's intention not to let such evil go unpunished (see the refrain in 5:9; 5:29; and 9:9, [in Hebrew, v. 8]). The ultimate cause of historical actions is God, and God is moved to care for God's people, both to bear their burdens and to punish their crimes.

Other poems in this anthology center on God's wrath. The prophet is called to be an instrument of that wrath of the Holy One, as in 5:14 where the words of the Holy One in his mouth are said to be fire that will consume "this people" who are wood. The importance of the prophet's role in the impending judgment of Judah is made clear by the poem about his role as an assayer of the quality of Judah's metal and accented by the poem's placement at the end of the section (6:27–30). The poem refers back to the call vision that begins the book, calling Jeremiah to be a prophet to the nations in order to "pluck up, pull down, destroy, and overthrow" (1:4–10). And it refers forward to the laments of the prophet in which he protests against the Holy One's abusive treatment of God's servant (11:18—12:6; 15:15–21; 17:14–18; 18:19–23; 20:7–18).

But the most dramatic poems in this collection deal with the terrible invasion that is soon to destroy the nation. Calls to flee, descriptions of agony, calls to attack, descriptions of mighty forces coming from the north, and anguished laments—all in the full color of shocking images and dramatic cries. Some of the most vigorous poetry in the whole book is found in these descriptions of the coming total collapse. One naturally asks, why such furious poetic descriptions of such terrible themes? The answer must be that many people had no sense of the impending calamity. The prophet must shock them into facing reality. There are those who say, "No evil will come upon us" (5:12). The prophets and the priests declare prosperity (*shalom*) when there is no real prosperity but only impending doom (6:13–14). One of the functions of the poet in any society is to shock people out of their complacency and awaken them to a sense of uncomfortable reality. Jeremiah, who knows his call to be fire to Judah's wood, rises to the occasion with some the most eloquent poetry of his time.

For convenience, I shall divide this anthology into three parts, corresponding to the chapter divisions in our Bibles. This should not obscure the fact that this is one collection that encompasses three chapters. Chapter 4 gathers some of the most shocking poetry about the impending disaster. Chapter 5 shifts the emphasis to the evils that provoke the Holy One's wrath, and chapter 6 contains poems where the presence of the prophet as herald of coming evils is more visible. But the collection is of one piece, and these are only relative emphases within a collection each of whose parts has some of each of the elements by which we characterize its various parts.

Terrible destruction is imminent (Jeremiah 4:5–31). This collection of poetry has very few or no specific referents, aside from the descriptions of the terrible invading armies (4:11–18) and the mention of the north as the direction from which the invasion will come (4:6). The main force of these poems is their shock value: Flee (4:6)! Put on sackcloth (4:8)! Anguish makes the walls of my (apparently, the Holy One's) heart writhe in pain (4:19)! The heavens grow black and the earth is stricken (4:28). A woman in childbirth cries out, gasping for breath (4:31). The prophet looks all around and sees nothing but desolation (4:23–26).

The need for such a "shock therapy" derives from the fact that the rulers and religious leaders are caught completely off guard. They think all is well (6:13–14). Even Jeremiah himself accuses the Holy One of deceiving this people and Jerusalem, having said they shall have peace when "the sword is at the throat" (4:10). It is possible to look at the same world and draw very different, indeed, opposite conclusions. There is a sector of the world's population that delights in the marvels of technical advances and feels that it lives in the best time in history. Yet, life expectancy in Africa has dropped drastically in the last decades and is now approaching forty years. In most countries of the world, the International Monetary Fund (IMF) imposes "structural adjustment" programs that lead to a growth in the economy but a depressing increase in the numbers of people with no access to any market commodities. Shopping centers go up in capital cities, surrounded by depressed areas where children die of infections that are not treated because, though doctors may prescribe antibiotics, mothers cannot afford to buy them.

Pastors in the pockets of comfort that still exist in today's sick world often preach a "gospel" of comfort that has no contact with the real world. They live in a dream world where growth has no limits and where the diseases and problems that surface occasionally can find technological solutions, given the marvels of modern science and technology. With regard to the real economy, politics, and religion, they suffer from a "reality crisis." In such a society, poets are speakers of reality, who name the comfort pockets for what they are, deceitful sectors protected by military might and a self-induced ignorance about a world in which millions of human beings perish from such "obsolete" illnesses as cholera or tuberculosis, that pose no threat at all to persons with access to clean water and modern drugs.

In Jeremiah's poetry, the Holy One speaks most of the time, calling unnamed persons (plural) to blow the trumpet to warn of the evil that is coming (4:5–8) or heralds to announce the coming of invaders (4:11–18), crying out in pain over the disaster that befalls the Holy One's stupid children (4:19–22), and then declaring that in spite of all this the Holy One, God, will not relent or turn back (4:27–28). The prophet himself takes a minor role, as the subject who looks all around for something that might survive the blight that assaults the land (4:23–26), and who accuses the Holy One of leading the people to a false confidence when there was no real peace (4:10).

Moral failure is to blame for the disaster (Jeremiah 5). The poems in this chapter are difficult to separate one from the next. They continue the theme of the imminent disaster and deal also with the role of the prophet as an agent of this disaster, but they focus especially on the evils of God's people. These evils have provoked the Holy One, who is ultimately responsible for the coming invasion.

The chapter opens with a call by the Holy One to some undefined people (plural) to run to and fro in Jerusalem and look for a person who "does justice and seeks fidelity" (5:1). One is reminded of the Cynic philosopher Diogenes of Sinope, who walked around Athens with his lamp at noon in search of an honest man. In the background, we should hear Abraham's appeal to the Holy One to spare Sodom if ten just persons should be found to reside within its borders (Gen. 18:32). The question is radicalized here: The Holy One will pardon Jerusalem if one such person be found. But instead, the people swear falsely (Jer. 5:2), refuse corrections from the Holy One (5:3), cater to those who are not gods (5:7), and commit adultery (5:7). The moral decay is found at all levels of society, from the rich to the poor (5:5). In the first appearance of a refrain that will be heard again, the

Holy One laments, "Upon a nation such as this shall I not bring retribution?" (5:9).

There is no doubt hyperbole here, as in the cases of Diogenes and Abraham. Did not at least Jeremiah do justice and seek fidelity? But we live in a time when it is practically impossible not to be involved with the exploitation of the poor of the world, if only through the actions of the banks and insurance companies who hold and manipulate our savings for retirement. We live in a culture that encourages us to look out for "number one" and prepares us to ignore the massive reality of poverty in our world. The poor are kept out of sight, and we are trained to avoid the places where we might encounter them and have to face reality. Solidarity is a word that now sounds archaic, no longer even a fighting call among today's labor unions. Yet, a small minority of today's world population lives in abundance while millions do not know how they will eat tomorrow. The "structural adjustment programs" that are imposed around the world are designed so that the poor of the world transfer daily enormous amounts to the banks where the comfortable and rich put their savings. Shall God not bring retribution on a world such as this?

Jeremiah 5:10–17 is a dramatic poem that contrasts the role of the prophets who are so much wind (5:13) with the role of Jeremiah as a fire set to the wood of the nation (5:14). When evil is an everyday reality, everywhere, it is hardly surprising if a people's prophets, preachers, and theologians have little to offer and are content to provide comforting rituals to people who no longer live with their feet on the ground, who look past men and women struggling for life in the face of death. If the role of God in such a time is to bring forth a mighty nation whose quivers are tombs (5:16; presumably a radicalizing touch from the editors, since this image is not found in the LXX), the role of the true prophet is to light the fire (5:14). But of course, God's people prefer the prophets who misrepresent reality with lies or with doctrines that fail to touch ground and pastors who rule their congregations on the instructions provided by these false prophets who are their theologians (5:31).

Jeremiah 5:20–29 is a dreadful indictment of God's people, who have eyes but no longer see their world, who have ears but no longer hear the cries of the needy. The lack of truth, the failure of a sense of reality lies with "your sins that have deprived you of the good" (5:25). Their houses are full of deceit/treachery, and thus have they grown rich (5:27). They are fat and sleek (the second word is uncertain in meaning in the Hebrew but the context gives a general sense; the phrase "fat and sleek" is missing in LXX and is perhaps a radicalization of the saying by later editors). But they do not make justice for the orphan or judge rightly the cause of the widow

(5:28). Here is the measure of a fully human society, the lives of its poor persons. A society that lacks means of life for the poor is an inhuman society! This is a clear and objective standard, but it gives failing marks to our world where growth seems to be the measuring stick, where the revolutions of our century are considered hopeless illusions, a world where politicians and economists say that there is no alternative to the Global Market. Again comes the haunting refrain, "On such a people, can I not bring retribution?" (5:29).

The prophet speaks to a people who do not wish to hear (Jeremiah 6). The poem in 6:1–8 is a cry by the Holy One for the Holy One's people, identified here as the children of Benjamin, to flee the destruction that impends from the north (6:1). Zion is a lovely pasture for armies that are likened to shepherds leading their flocks (6:2–3). (The image of the pasture is not in LXX, though the coming of the "shepherds" with their flocks is there; the poem has been improved by the editors.) In 6:4, we hear the battle cries of the armies of "shepherds" who lament the shortness of daylight for their destructive work. But in 6:6 the Holy One enters into the design of the attack, calling for the building of ramps to take the city: "This is the city that must be visited" (in biblical Hebrew, a "visitation" is usually a punishment for crimes committed). In this line, LXX suggests an alternative: "This is the city of falsehood (*polis pseudes*)." The poem concludes with a threat that the Holy One will make the city a desolation, an uninhabited place (6:8). Again, we are reminded that the identity of the mysterious invader from the north is unimportant because it is the Holy One who controls the movements of the armies of this world. For believers who live in the center of global might and whose sons serve as soldiers in the army and navy of empire or as scientists in the laboratories where weapons of mass destruction are designed and tested, it may seem unreal to speak of God as the ultimate actor in imperial history. But from the underside of history, the presence of God is real, for it is the source of a hope necessary to keep up the struggle for life. The theological problem for the underside is that it should be God who is behind armies that support a system that kills—kills not the perpetrators but their victims—on so massive a scale. Both believers at the heart of empire and believers who are victims of empire may have difficulty taking the prophet's verses seriously.

The prophet's dilemma comes through a bit more in the poem in 6:10–15. How can he continue to speak when the ears of the people are closed (literally, uncircumcised)? The prophet feels the full force of the Lord's anger and can no longer hold it. The Holy One demands that he "pour" it out upon children, youth, and aged persons (6:11). It helps, perhaps, that the prophet knows that all are moved by greed—the Hebrew says "they bite off bites," a crude way of speaking of the search for profit (6:13). In a city where each person, small or great, lives to make profit, the prophet and the priest become false (*sheqer*, one of Jeremiah's favorite words; of 119 uses of this word in the Hebrew Bible, 37 are in Jeremiah). They say, "peace and prosperity," when there is no *shalom*. The prosperity or wellbeing or peace (*shalom*) has become a lie, *sheqer*, because the Holy One has been angered. It cannot persist. One thinks of the ways in which participation in the so-called "good" life leads so many to be oblivious to the damage that this kind of life causes to millions whose potential wealth is drained by the financial manipulation of debts and investments, not to mention the atmosphere and the forests and the rivers of our world. Poetry and prophecy seek to unmask the unreality of what is considered daily reality by those who benefit by "biting" and whose vested interest puts blinders on their eyes.

The next poem, 6:16–21, adds to the indictment in the previous poems a new piece of information: The people of God who are being judged and condemned are a religious people who bring burnt offerings and sacrifices. But these will not deflect their calamity, because they "have not given heed to my words" (6:19–20). The words that have been ignored are precisely the warnings of the poets whom God sent as sentinels to sound the trumpet of alarm (6:17). (In Hebrew, which distinguishes singular and plural forms of "you," it is clear that verse 16, which invites a plural subject to stand on the roads and ask for the ancient ways, is not talking to the prophet but to the people.)

In such a situation of unreality, where a people lives in ignorance of its own moral decay and the threat that menaces its very survival, the prophet takes on a heightened importance. The whole collection on the impending disaster, 4:5—6:30, ends with a brief reflection on the prophet as a tester of metals (6:27–30) whose tests reveal only base metals where noble ones were expected. The whole ends with the damning verdict, "They are called Rejected Silver because the Holy One has rejected them." In a situation where gross injustice has caused general deception as to the nature of reality, prophets who "see through" the veil of injustice become indispensable to the survival of the people!

PART D

Rejection of God's Word
(Jeremiah 7—10)

━━━━━━━━━━━━━━━━━━━━━

These four chapters of the book of Jeremiah are not as tightly knit as the previous three. Yet, a common thread runs through the prose and poetry gathered here, and that thread has to do with how the "true religion" of the Holy One has been converted into a lie by the injustices committed by the worshiping community against the poor in their midst. The collection begins with a prose version of Jeremiah's famous "Temple Sermon" (7:2–15) and concludes with a poem that is a satire on idolatry. In the collection of poems gathered in between, in chapters 8 and 9, the topic of false religion prevails. In the ring structure of the book, Jeremiah 7—10 corresponds to a prose section, Jeremiah 34—38, that describes various particular episodes of rejection of the Holy One's word. Of course, when reading a book, one moves from the beginning to the end and therefore the ring structure only appears after the middle, when it invites the reader to go back and look again. Hence, when we arrive at that later section, the reader will be invited to come back and look again at this one.

"A Den of Thieves Have You Made of This House" (Jeremiah 7:1—8:3)

This is the "Temple Sermon," which, according to the Christian gospels, Jesus quoted during one of his visits to the Jerusalem temple (Mt. 21:13;

Mk. 11:17; Lk. 19:45). Although its literary-historical problems have been solved in different ways, this text must be given an important place in any reading of the book of Jeremiah. This is one of the book's clearest statements of Jeremiah's accusations against his people, accusations that ground the judgment leading to a threat of military attacks from the north. At the heart of the accusations is the falsehood (*sheqer*) in the life of the nation Judah. Judah builds its self-deceiving falsehood on truth, the truth of the Holy One's revelation that the Name will reside on Jerusalem's holy temple hill and on the practice of the sacrifices and festivals that the Holy One ordained for the people on another mountain, Sinai, in the days of Moses. Through theft, murder, adultery, false oaths, and wrong sacrifices, the true religion of Israel has become falsehood in the very house in which the Holy One's Name resides.

Before looking at this master text more closely, we must look at some issues of style and location. This is a prose text in a homiletic (preaching) style that will recur in several other places in the book of Jeremiah (Jer. 11:1–13; 18:1–12; 21:1–10; 25:1–14; 34:8–22; 35:1–19). The style of these "sermons" differs in important ways from the book's poetry and shows affinities with the so-called "Deuteronomistic" style of the books from Deuteronomy through 2 Kings. The core message of the book of Jeremiah is laid out in these sermons that deal with the word of God and of God's messengers, the prophets. The sermon's style is very close to the narrative style of other passages in the book of Jeremiah that begin to appear in chapter 26 and include all of chapters 36—44.

Without trying to resolve all the problems of the composition of the book of Jeremiah, let us read with the following assumptions: (1) Jeremiah was probably the composer of most of the poetry. (2) He did not write the narrative passages in which he is the main character. These likely came from scribes of the *golah*, the community that took shape in the Babylonian exile. These scribes would have given the book its present form. (3) While the sermons are difficult to place in the history of the shaping of the book, they seem closer to the editorial narratives than to the words of the prophet himself. While we cannot be absolutely certain about the book's history, these observations and assumptions will help us to understand its diversity.

In other words, the book we have in the Bible is obviously the result of a process of editing, most clearly evident when we look at the ancient Greek translation (LXX) and its variations from our canonical Hebrew text (MT). We must take account of the distance between the poetry and the prose in some way. It seems likely that respectful scribes who considered themselves to be followers of Jeremiah put the book together out of Jeremiah's own poetry, some prose sermons probably based on statements he made, and narratives that give a historical setting for the whole. We might compare the situation to the development of Christian faith traditions such as the Methodist, Baptist, Anglican, and Roman Catholic. Each tradition has a great internal diversity and yet is recognizable. One Roman Catholic recognizes another, even if one is shaped within the Franciscan spiritual current and another by the Jesuit one. For a Methodist, John Wesley holds a special place, even though the difference between a Methodist social activist and a Methodist "evangelical" may be considerable. The sermons are probably very close to Jeremiah in spirit, if not in the language, but perhaps even in much of the language. Here, we have a Charles Wesley as compared to his brother John Wesley or a George Whitefield to John Wesley, the same message though in a style that may not be that of the master.

There is obviously a close connection between Jeremiah's Temple Sermon and the narrative contained in chapter 26. This narrative tells of the reaction to the sermon, how the prophet narrowly escaped being killed by "the priests and the prophets and all the people" who heard him speaking (Jer. 26:7). Court officials, in particular Ahikam the son of Shaphan, save the day for Jeremiah (Jer. 26:10; 26:24). Thus we discover that there existed within the royal court a sector favorable to Jeremiah and his vision for the future of Judah. At its core was the influential family of descendants of the scribe Shaphan, who had assisted Josiah in his great reform (2 Kings 22:8–14, presumably in the early days of Jeremiah's ministry). Gedaliah, a son of Ahikam and grandson of Shaphan, would be appointed governor of Judah by Nebuchadnezzar (an alternate spelling of this name, Nebuchadrezzar, appears in many chapters of Jeremiah) after the destruction of Jerusalem (Jer. 40:11), and Jeremiah would support him in this political project. But as we read Jeremiah 7, we do not yet know this. So, let us return to the sequence of the book.

According to the Hebrew text of Jeremiah 7:1–2, the prophet is ordered to proclaim the word of the Holy One at the temple gate to those who are coming through the gate with the intention of worshiping there. This specific setting is missing in the LXX, which introduces the sermon with "Hear the word of the Lord, all of Judah" and moves right into the sermon at verse 3. A comparison with chapter 26 shows that both deal with the same message and, also, that the editors have taken the setting for the sermon in Jeremiah 7:1–2 from 26:2. The resulting text is clearer than LXX or, as we would say today, is more reader-friendly. We are told that the prophet's hearers are pious people come to worship at the temple. This is important for the reader, even if she or he does not yet know the violent reaction Jeremiah's words will provoke (chap. 26). When we hear that the sermon was pronounced at the gate, we should remember that there was no regular time set for a sermon. Worship was held in the courtyard and centered on the slaughter and burning of animals in the area of the altar. We can imagine curious worshipers gathering as the prophet stood or sat on a "soapbox" to give his message.

The sermon is directed against precisely the people who, during their pilgrimage to the temple, gather to listen. It is they who have committed the evils listed in 7:9 and have then come to the temple to "be saved" at the place where the Holy One's Name is invoked (7:10). It is these pious people who have made the house where the Holy One's Name is invoked into a den of thieves (7:11), a cave where thieves hide from the police and conceal their loot.

Jeremiah's role is different from that of a modern preacher. He does not have a congregation to whom he must deliver weekly capsules of God's word. A congregation like the ones we know today would not long tolerate a pastor who preached like Jeremiah. Nor would regular sermons like his be tolerated in Jerusalem. Jeremiah, though of priestly lineage (Jer. 1:1), was not part of the temple personnel. He appeared at the temple gate one day or two as an outsider and, like the speechmaker on the proverbial soapbox, gave his sermon to an audience of strangers, after which he and they returned to their routine activities. Jeremiah did not make his living preaching the word of God.

This raises some questions about how we institutionalize the word of God. Institutions such as church congregations are necessary to create a place for religion in our societies. But if God is to send "God's servants the prophets persistently" to speak the word (Jer. 7:13, 25; 25:4; 26:5; 29:19; 35:14–15), they must speak from a less vulnerable location than the local pulpit. Do we have such locations in our societies? One thinks of the positions of professors of theology in our seminaries and universities. Academic tenure was designed to provide the protection necessary to speak the undesired word that might be the word of God. Unfortunately, tenure is rapidly becoming a thing of the past as universities are hiring on more provisional bases, arguing that tenured professors easily become fossils out of touch with current trends. There is some truth to this, but it leaves the prophet exposed to impossible pressures. One might think of news commentators in great newspapers or television news programs. But it is evident that these news channels of our society are today in the hands of big business, and they have a limited tolerance for critical perspectives on social order.

Prophets have always had to find niches, cracks, in society where the word of God can find a place. And the prophet is ever exposed. One thinks of the murders of Malcolm X, Martin Luther King Jr., and Archbishop

Oscar Arnulfo Romero in the twentieth century. And of course, of Jesus himself, Stephen, Peter, and Paul in the first century, Ignatius, Justin, and Polycarp in the second. Still, a healthy society requires some guarantees for its prophets. The emergence of human rights organizations like Amnesty International is surely a good sign, and one cannot doubt that many prophets have been granted more time by the existence of these organizations.

Jeremiah 7 contains many surprises. Verse 16 forbids the prophet to pray for his people. Verses 21–24 sarcastically invite the people to offer sacrifices and enjoy the meat from them but not to imagine that the Holy One enjoys the meat offered by people who have no ears for the word of their God. Jeremiah goes so far as to say that the Holy One never asked for sacrifices in the desert when bringing the people out of Egypt (7:22), a surprising statement that reminds us of Amos 5:25 but which runs contrary to Leviticus 1—7 and many other Sinaitic laws. We are also reminded of Isaiah's strictures (Isa. 1:10–17), which condemn sacrifices accompanied by injustice. Amos and Jeremiah seem to know some traditions about the Sinai that differ from the ones preserved in our Pentateuch. In any case, the relevant contrast is sacrifice and prayer, on the one hand, and obedience to the word of the Holy One on the other. The word has to do with justice for the stranger, the widow, and the orphan (Jer. 7:6), which brings Jeremiah close to Isaiah.

Jeremiah's words radically relativize all forms of worship. The Holy One will not listen to the prayers and hymns of people who do not obey God's word, even though they believe they are being obedient (7:16). The prophet's audience truly believes that the Temple is holy, and it is only the prophet who realizes that their actions out in the streets have profaned it. There is a lesson to be learned, says Jeremiah, from the destruction or abandonment of the temple at Shiloh where Samuel was raised centuries before (7:13–15; compare 1 Sam. 1—4). If the Holy One abandoned Shiloh to its dreadful destiny, why should God not do the same for the Jerusalem temple? Or, for a nation that in the 1890s supported imperial designs with pious reflections on Manifest Destiny and which today proclaims on its dollar bills "In God we trust" while bombing the people of Hiroshima, Viet Nam, Iraq, Kosovo, and Afghanistan? Like the ancient Judeans, we have convinced ourselves that this is what God demands. This is false consciousness, ideology, *sheqer*.

This passage ends with a threat to turn Jerusalem into a cemetery and a place of mourning (7:29—8:3). This no longer appears to be part of the Temple Sermon, which seems to end at 7:15, but it fits with the message of that sermon and it links that sermon with the poetic blasts gathered in chapters 4—6. Piety cannot save a nation that no longer has ears for the word of God. This message remains important for nations that consider themselves Christian but undertake world domination without consulting the will of other peoples or the word of God.

The Holy One Denounces the People, Lays Them Waste, and Cries over Them (Jeremiah 8:4—9:26)

As in chapters 2—6, we have God's speech cast in poetic form, except for the short prose pieces in 9:12–16 and 9:23–24. (The Hebrew versification differs by one verse throughout chapter 9: English 9:2 is Hebrew 9:1.) The dominant note of this "God-poetry" is the accusation that God's people have practiced deceit and become false. They have gone astray and, unlike the stork or the swallow, which return in due season to their homes, they are not aware of the situation and do not return (8:4–6). They are like a horse plunging into battle who loses his sense of direction in the confusion (8:6).

"From small to great all pursue their own gain" (8:10); the priest and the prophet act falsely. In a wise editorial move, the MT inserts here (8:11–12) some lines from 6:14–15 that sum up the falsehood of the religious leaders: They trivialize the wound of the people, saying, "Peace, Peace [or Prosperity, Prosperity]" when there is no peace.

At certain points in the sequence of these chapters, we hear the laments of those stricken by the Holy One's punishment. "Let us gather into the fortified cities and perish there; for the Holy God has caused us to perish...We sought peace but found no good, a time of healing, but there was terror instead" (8:15). "The harvest is past. Summer is over. But we are not saved" (8:20). Sometimes, the prophet seems to speak for his own person: "My heart is sick. Hark, the sounds of the grief of the daughter of my people coming from a distant land" (8:18–19). "Who would make me a head of waters, my eyes a fountain of tears, that I might weep day and night for the slain of the daughter of my people" (9:1). "Over the hills I will raise weeping and laments, and over the pastures a dirge, for they are deserted so that none passes by, and the lowing of cattle is not heard; both the birds of the heavens and the animals have fled and are gone" (9:10).

But mostly we have words delivered in the voice of the Holy One, sometimes accusations, sometimes decrees of destruction, and sometimes sorrow over the people. Apparently, it is the Holy One who laments: "Who can provide me in the desert a hotel by the way, and I would leave my people and go away from them! They are all disloyal [adulterers], a band of traitors" (9:2). "Therefore thus says the Holy God Sabaoth, I am refining and testing them, what else could I do with the daughter of my people?

Their tongue is a murderous arrow, their mouths speak deceit, uttering peaceful expressions to their neighbors while planning in their interior an ambush" (9:7–8). The sad refrain in Jeremiah 9:9 repeats Jeremiah 5:9 and 5:29 and thus ties together the collection about the threat from the north (chapters 4—6) with the collection on the falsehood of society (chapters 7—10).

What are we to make of this strange speech? This is not a sermon or a coherent speech. It is a string of poems put in the mouth of the Holy One, interspersed with utterances of the terrified people or the distressed prophet. Poetry here plays an indispensable social role. It is not bound by the canons of "rational" language. The poet uses strange language to take distance from socially approved "order." The Holy One can in poetry say outlandish things that the well-trained God of the liturgy and the pulpit would not be caught dead uttering. The heart of the poet can be sick with apprehension (8:18) while the words heard in the pulpits of the land soothe the believers with assurances of peace and prosperity (8:11).

We are reminded that in Plato's perfect city philosophers were kings, soldiers protected the perfect order designed by "seekers of wisdom," and skilled workers built the houses and implements needed by all, while slaves did the dirty work. But poets were forbidden because they were not constrained by "truth," the official science discovered and proclaimed by the wise philosophers. Homer and his kin care little for the truth: They tell stories of gods who rant and rave in their fury. They are not careful to preserve the honor of the city's heroes. Not only do the poets have little respect for the truth, they are dangerous because the fictions they conjure up are adorned in beautiful language that seduces the unguarded among the youth. According to Plato's *Republic* (Books II and X), poets are dangerous for a well-ordered city. This ought to be an eye-opener. If poets are so dangerous to social control, they must have an important social role to play if a society is to remain human.

We can understand why prophecy and poetry seem inseparably intertwined. It is not possible to speak of God or the gods within the parameters required by the "truth" that rules the political and economic sciences of ordered social life. The word of God comes from outside this well-ordered reality. The prophet/poet must take leave of ordinarily accepted language, even the language ordinarily accepted in the pulpit, if he or she is to speak for God. God just doesn't fit within this ordered reality. But if reality is to remain honest and be true to what is human, it also requires the distance that only poetry can provide. So, we understand why the prophets take up poetry to say what ordinary science does not see about reality. Much of what is most important to the well-being and persistence of society can only be spoken outside of the parameters of accepted scientific or religious language. So, we have the outrageous posture of the man from Anathoth who dares to speak God's word in a self-satisfied society that feels it knows anything God might want to say and doesn't need a poetic prophet.

Is it a reflection on U.S. society that poetry is so marginal to national life? Could our churches become centers for the production and/or diffusion of poetry? Could our schools stage recitals of poetry and contests among aspiring poets? What about the place of poetry in our newspapers?

A Prose Explanation (Jeremiah 9:12–16)

The prose section in 9:12–16 (Hebrew, 9:11–15) appears to attempt to explain the heavy poetry in more readily acceptable terms. Both the LXX and MT place this prose right after some very strong poetic statements in which the Holy One calls for lamentation because Jerusalem will be made into a heap of ruins and Judah a desolation without inhabitant (9:10–11). Now comes the direct prose question, "Who is the man wise enough to understand this? Why will the land be laid ruin with none to pass through it?" (9:12). The answer is spelled out in straightforward and sober language in 9:13–14—they have forsaken my law, not obeyed my voice, and worshiped Baal. This is a "religious" explanation, much more so than the poetry, which mentioned neither the law nor the god Baal. One feels the attempt to reduce the drastic threats of the poetry to terms that can be understood by pious people.

The "therefore" conclusion in 9:15–16 starts by picking up the striking grief of a people who feel poisoned by their God (8:14). In the poetry, the people blamed God for their destruction; now God gives a pondered judgment for the sins mentioned. Verse 16 introduces the punishment of exile, revealing the hand of the editors who were living in or had just returned from Babylon.

The book Jeremiah includes both the striking poetry we have examined in 8:4—9:11 and the more pondered theological reflection of 9:12–16 in both LXX, which I take to be the earlier edition, and in MT, which I take to be somewhat later. The book was written for a generation for which the destruction announced in the poetry lay in the past. That generation's task was to preserve and interpret the poetry for the construction of a new Judah under Persian hegemony. We at the outset of the twenty-first century are not in such a moment of new construction but in a time more like that of Jeremiah's original audience, a moment of apparent peace when there is no real peace. Yet, we can benefit from remembering that the Scriptures both reveal crude reality, as in the poetry, and help to build new reality, as in this prose meditation.

The Holy One Is to Be Known as a Merciful God
(Jeremiah 9:23–24)

The measured prose of 9:23–24 has some of the rhythm of poetry but is closer to a theological reflection of the sort we would expect from the book's editors. After all the terrorizing poetry in 8:4—9:22, it is something of a tour de force to say, as does the Holy One here, that "I act with mercy, justice, and right upon the earth." But it is, of course, not possible to build a religious community on the experience of God who gives poisoned water to drink (8:14) or causes corpses to cover the fields like dung (9:22). Somehow, the dreadful experience of the destruction of the temple and the capital city and the death and exile of its population must be understood in theologically acceptable terms if a new life is to be built. Here Jeremiah's editors come to the rescue, at the risk of toning down the full force of the prophet's message.

The Holy One, the God of Israel, Surpasses All Other Gods
(Jeremiah 10:1–16)

The introduction to this piece (10:1–2) gives its intention: It warns Israel to resist being seduced by the gods of the nations. This gives context for a piece that we might be tempted to read as cheap sarcasm against the faith of peoples who find comfort in praying before shrines centered on images. It is true that Israel practiced a cult that was mostly devoid of graven or molten images. Nevertheless, the prohibition of representations was not total as it was to be later in Muslim law and practice. At the heart of the Jerusalem temple were carved images, overlaid with gold, of two winged lions or bulls known as cherubim (1 Kings 6:23–28). In the temple courtyard stood a bronze sea for washing up in connection with the sacrifices. It was mounted on twelve bulls (1 Kings 7:23–25). The walls of the temple were covered with cedar that had carved images of cherubim, palm trees, and open flowers (1 Kings 6:29). The doors of the entrance were also adorned with carved cherubim, palm trees, and flowers (1 Kings 6:33–35).

So, we should not understand this section of Jeremiah as an attack on the use of images as such. It does not have to do with purifying Israelite worship. The issue is rather the temptation to look to the gods of the other nations—specifically, in the context of the Babylonian exile, the gods of Babylon. These gods were ornately made out of precious silver and gold, clothed in fine cloth by the best weavers of the world (10:4, 8–9). The victories of Babylonian armies could be taken as evidence for the power of these gods. One can imagine young people and some elders as well feeling the attraction of such success. The poet begins and ends his reflections on these gods by calling them *hevel*, vapor, nothing (10:3, 15). Their attraction is *sheqer*, falsehood (10:14).

So why are the gods of the nations *hevel* while Israel's Holy One is incomparable? Because the gods are the product of human crafting and can do nothing (10:3–5), while the Holy One is "the living God and everlasting King" (10:10) who "made the earth by his might" (10:12). Here we have the crux of the issue of idolatry: It is infatuation with the creations of human ingenuity, leading to the illusion that humans can do anything and that we reign supreme over and above the rest of the creatures.

Who can doubt that human science and technology have wrought marvels? Humans have walked on the moon. They fly across the oceans in just a few hours. In the wealthy nations of the world, houses have heating and cooling devices that maintain an ideal climate all year around in the severest of regions. Some people protest that the environment is being destroyed by the toxic discards of luxurious living, but many are confident that science will resolve these problems just as it solved others. While youth in the rich sliver of the world's population enjoy undreamed-of luxury, most of the world's population experiences an explosion of misery. Is not this impressive human achievement really *hevel* and *sheqer*?

Karl Marx believed that the religion of modernity is the worship of Capital. Having discovered the secret of unlimited accumulation after inventing money and after the removal of the general population from the land where they could produce their own livelihood without selling their work to others, everything was now submitted to the idol that seemed capable of multiplying itself without limits. Traditional religion had become a mere survival of older times, because the driving force of today's world was money that made money, Capital. But of course, there is a fly in the ointment. Capital—cars, air conditioners, luxurious mansions, covered stadiums—is all "dead labor," the work of years past, but it becomes the driving force of today's living people. A vast system of credit locks the average person, who derives much from this humanly produced god, into service to that god. Once one is hooked on credit, there is no leaving the ship, even if we see the iceberg looming on the horizon. An idol is not a pure illusion. Jeremiah never claims that false gods don't exist. Because they exist and because they have fascination, they are dangerous and must be rejected. The ultimate sin is apostasy, abandoning the flowing waters of the living God for the humanly hewn cisterns of false gods that cannot retain the water they collect (Jer. 2:13).

The structure of Jeremiah 10's tirade against the seductive false gods of the nations is ABABABAB, where A represents the critique of the false gods of the nations and B the praise of the Holy One, the "portion" of Israel. The point is driven home by a fourfold reiteration, not very elegant poetry, perhaps, but certainly forceful. In lieu of the center that a ring structure would have provided, Jeremiah 10:11 stands out by being written in Aramaic, an official language of the Babylonian empire: "Thus shall you (plural) say to them: The gods who didn't make the heavens and the earth shall perish from the earth and from under these heavens [that is, the real heavens made by the Holy One]."

In the LXX, which probably represents a more ancient edition of the Hebrew, this poetic tirade looks quite different. The poem is shorter, lacking verses 6–8 of the MT, which comprise a full B section (praise of the Holy One) and part of an A section (mockery of the other gods). MT's verse 9, the rest of that A section, is located in the LXX between verses 4 and 5, making it part of a longer A section. The result in LXX is a ring structure, which, using the Hebremnd English) numbering, goes as follows:

Introduction (vv. 1–2)

   Mockery of the gods of the nations (vv. 3–4, 9, 5)

      A threat to the false gods (v. 11)

   Praise of the Holy One as creator (vv. 12–13)

A conclusion on foolishness and implied wisdom (vv. 14–16)

Although the poetry is not well-wrought (well-wrought poetry is hard to achieve in this sarcastic mode), the LXX's arrangement is elegant. In the center stands the threat to the false gods, which in MT is marked out by its Aramaic language; this is a phrase emphasized by both, then, although by different editorial techniques.

The differences between our two versions in a poetic piece no doubt indicate that this is a composition of the Jeremiah tradition from the Babylonian exile and does not go back to the preexilic prophet. The piece may well have come from the same group that did Isa. 44:9–20, which is quite similar in tone and images and also seems to have come from Babylonian exiles. It was difficult to ridicule gods who seemed to be in power. We have the same difficulty today in exposing the falsity of the seemingly triumphant god Capital. From Babylon, it was not at all obvious that the gods of the nations were worthless, and, from comfortable communities, it is not evident that Capital is a false god with feet of clay.

Punish, but Not in Anger (Jeremiah 10:17–25)

The long collection that has to do somehow with the threat from the north closes with a call to pack for departure (Jer. 10:17), for the noise from the north is approaching (10:22). The people are thrust out of the land and their tents destroyed (10:18, 20). The person of the prophet appears as the poem draws to a close in Jeremiah 10:24–25. He speaks to God as one of the people who are suffering the invasion and consequent destruction. As a believer, he expresses willingness to accept punishment but as an act of justice and not anger (10:24). He closes with an appeal to the Holy One to consider that the evils of the nations are greater than those of Judah, and yet "they have devoured Jacob" (10:25). With this poem, the editors close this portion of the book and prepare for the next one, chapters 11 to 20, where the person of the prophet will play a more prominent role.

Covenant Suspended:
The Prophet's Impossible Role
(Jeremiah 11—20)

Jeremiah 11—20 deals with suspension of the nation's covenant with God (Jer. 11:1–17) and the impossible position in which this places the prophet (11:18—20:18). These chapters correspond, in the ring structure of Jeremiah, to chapters 30—33, which speak of a new covenant and new prophetic role.

The Holy One's People Have Violated Their Covenant
(Jeremiah 11:1–17)

This section has two parts: a prose passage in 11:1–14 and poetic verses in 11:15–17. They share the motif of the people's disobedience to the demands of the Holy One, demands formulated as a covenant with the ancestors when God brought them out of the "iron furnace" in Egypt. The overall message is clear: The covenant was broken by the ancestors, and the damage is irreparable. The prophet must bear this hopeless message to a people who at this moment have no future.

It is important to situate this passage within the canonical book of Jeremiah (the MT). It echoes the Temple Sermon in 7:1–15. That passage and this one both call for conduct that is more than ritual correctness. The Temple Sermon, however, calls for repentance, a turning that would change the conduct of the people. In our text, the time for repentance has been exhausted. Repentance is now a lost possibility, exile an irreversable fate. On the other hand, within the ring structure of canonical Jeremiah, 11:1–17 corresponds to 31:32—33:26, the offer of a new covenant. The latter text envisions a future for the chastened people who have returned from exile, or, in the Christian reading of it, for the people who build their community on Jesus Christ (2 Cor. 3:4–8 and Heb. 8:8–12). In any case, the message of the book is that the people of the Holy One do have a future, but that future can only be built on acceptance of God's punishment and a newness of life.

In the more immediate context, the failure of the people to "hear" the call of the Holy One prepares for the refusal on the part of God to hear the prayers of the people, a motif that is prominent in chapters 14 and 15 in connection with a drought.

The curse on those who disobey the commands of the covenant (Jeremiah 11:1–5). The passage opens with the Holy One's command to the prophet to pronounce a curse on those who do not "hear," that is, obey, the words of the covenant. This is a reference, first of all, to the curses pronounced by Moses in Moab after reading the laws given by the Holy One at Sinai (Deut. 27—28). The curses comprise a spine-tingling list of horrific evils that can be expected by a people disobedient to the Holy One's covenant demands. The prophet is now sent by the Holy One to remind "the people of Judah and the inhabitants of Jerusalem" of the curses that their ancestors pronounced on themselves in the event they failed to perform the acts the Holy One imposed on them.

Jeremiah 11:4 gives the basis for this covenant with the ancestors: the salvific deeds of the Holy One. The commands were given and accepted after the Holy One "had brought them out of the land of Egypt out of the iron furnace." The formula "bring out of Egypt" occurs 83 times in the Bible, mostly in legal texts but never in the books of the prophets of the 700s B.C.E.[1] It is often, as in this case, the foundation for a call to obedience to the laws given at Sinai. An alternative formula, "brought up from the land of Egypt," occurs forty-one times, several of them in Amos, Hosea, and Micah, prophets of the 700s B.C.E. It is often associated with the entry into the promised land (Ex. 3:8, 17; Gen. 50:24, and others). Perhaps the migration seemed the important thing about the exodus to people who still dwelt securely in their land, while departure from slavery was the most interesting point for the writers of the legal materials and in the post-586 texts. In any case, Jeremiah unambiguously presents freedom from oppression (the "iron furnace") as the foundation of the covenant. We should also see in the iron furnace a reference to the iron yoke that Jeremiah assumes, later in the book, as symbol of the punishment his people can expect (28:13). The Holy One brought them out of the iron furnace, but the people have chosen the curse of an iron yoke, which is how Jeremiah views their necessary submission to the Babylonians.

The intention of the Holy One was that "you would be my people and I would be your God" (Jer. 11:4). This solemn formula occurs frequently in the books of Jeremiah and Ezekiel (see, for instance, Jer. 7:23; 24:7; 30:22; 31:33; 32:38; and Ezek. 11:20; 14:11; 36:28) and in a somewhat different form in Hosea 2:23. Deuteronomy has the half of the formula that deals with the Holy One as God of Israel (Deut. 26:17–18; 27:9; 28:9), though of course the other half is implicit. It is a powerful expression of the nature of the people Israel!

As Christians, we call ourselves the body of Christ (Rom. 12:5; 1 Cor. 12:27; Eph. 1:22–23, and others). This is a way of imagining a community that is God's and a God who is the community's. Our Christian relation has its obligations just as did the covenant of the Holy One with Israel. Paul observes that it is not right to make the members of Christ members of a whore (1 Cor. 6:15–20). In his farewell to his own in Galilee, the risen Christ imposes on them the obligation to teach the nations to keep "all that I have commanded you" (Mt. 28:20). In the same appearance, Christ promises to be with them always until the end of the world. This presence is not obvious, however. Jesus in the flesh has finished his teaching with a vision of the final judgment, where believer and nonbeliever discover whether they have been with Christ or not. The surprise for both is that Christ's presence is incarnate in the needy now that he is no longer with them in his own flesh (Mt. 25:31–46). We Christians can read Jeremiah 11 as a curse on us if we fail to recognize Christ among us in the poor and needy, who in the twentieth century became and today still are Legion, especially in the so-called Third World.

The bringing out from Egypt is linked in Jeremiah 11 with entry into "the land that flows with milk and honey" (11:5, a rare linkage in the Bible as a whole). Remember that our book is addressed to a people who have lost their land, so the "as of this day" in verse 5 refers backward to their past, when they enjoyed freedom from slavery and possession of a land that flowed with milk and honey (a traditional expression found in Ex. 3:8, 17; 13:5; 33:3; Num. 13:27; 14:8; Deut. 6:3, and others). This fertile situation will be shortly turned on its head in the drought of chapters 14–15 of Jeremiah. So, the book is addressed to a people who have lost both their freedom (to Babylon) and their land (to exile). Jeremiah 11:1–14 reminds them that their immediate ancestors had a chance to repent when the Holy One sent Jeremiah to them to remind them of the curse under which they lived.

Jeremiah sent again but ignored by Judah and Jerusalem (Jeremiah 11:6–8). Jeremiah was sent again to proclaim in the cities of Judah and the streets of Jerusalem the need to "hear" the words of the covenant. The appeal is not just based on the exodus and Sinai events but on the consistent calls of the prophets whom the Holy One had persistently sent to the present day. But "you did not hear" and so the Holy One brought the curses down on the people. Here a comparison of LXX with MT is instructive. LXX does not have any of verses 7–8 except the last phrase, "and they did not do it." Our canonical Jeremiah (MT) is a revised text, as is clearly shown by the fact that the verses under discussion seem to be an addition of MT (and not an omission of LXX) in order to make clear to the exilic community that the curse is already taking its effect and the time for conversion is past. This is probably also the intention of the earlier version reflected in LXX, but it is made explicit in the later edition of the text. It would appear that the Christian church is not yet at the point where the curse takes effect, certainly not in the manner in which the exilic readers of Jeremiah understood it. Although empire is here, and though the church is in part in the "belly of the beast," to use José Marti's expression, the empire is still perceived as a friendly one, as was the Roman empire to Luke in the Acts of the Apostles. The effects of this unholy alliance are not yet evident.

Because they have not "heard," neither will the Holy One (11:9–14). Again, the prophet receives a message for Judah and Jerusalem: A "conspiracy" has been found out (11:9–10). This is a surprising development. The conspiracy is a widespread practice of appealing to the gods of the land because the people have turned away from the Holy One. The image of a "conspiracy," something that is not easily seen but must be ferreted out, is ambiguous both for Judah and for the church today. A conspiracy is something a group works out consciously in secret. But Judah's problem, and the church's today, is not a conscious plan, because they and we are just as deceived as the outsiders. Judah and the church are not aware of their idolatry, which they conceal from themselves. Christians are today, by and large, part and parcel of the larger society that worships Capital, money that engenders money by buying raw materials, producing and selling goods. As with Judah, there is a guilty conscience about the false gods, but no clarity about the demands of the covenant or the obligations of being the body of Christ. Jeremiah 10 has just presented the reader with a satire on idolatry where the conspiracy is not yet evident. The conspiracy involved is not conscious concealment so much as half-conscious self-deception. Only so does Jeremiah's application of the idea of a conspiracy make sense, but, read thus, it does indeed make sense!

As a result of the people's failure to "hear" the demands of the covenant, the Holy One will now refuse to "hear" the prayers of the people of Judah (11:11). The covenant is broken, for there is no longer any communication!

In Jeremiah 11:14, the prophet is instructed to cease praying for this people, because the Holy One will no longer listen to intercession on their behalf. For believers, this is a disconcerting prohibition. A servant of God cannot obey it. Our model is Moses, who stood up to the Holy One's "last word on Israel" at the incident of the golden calf (Ex. 32:7–14). Religion becomes pointless if we can't pray. God's instruction to the prophet is dramatic evidence of the depth of the *sheqer*—then and perhaps now. We will hear more about this in the next section.

The Prophet's Impossible Role (Jeremiah 11:18—20:18)

We have just read a devastating statement by the Holy One that the covenant between God and Israel is over and can no longer be renewed. The wicked acts of Israel have forced God to a terrible decision to cancel all relations. What more can possibly be said in such a circumstance? Is there any point in continuing a prophetic ministry when the story is finished? It would seem not. And yet, the book of Jeremiah is not an epitaph. Nor is the book finished. Far from it, most of the book is still ahead of us. Obviously, after Jeremiah 11:17, things must look very different from what one would expect in normal times—but how?

The next, rather large section of Jeremiah deals with the impossible role of the Holy One's prophet after the covenant has been cancelled by divine decree in response to Israel's continuous evil actions. It opens and closes with two of the five "confessions" of Jeremiah, prayers of the prophet to which God responds. There is a certain progression. The first prayer, Jeremiah 11:18–23, takes place in the context of a plot to murder the prophet. Acquaintances from Jeremiah's home town are involved. Jeremiah knows that the motive is not personal. The plotters are responding logically to the terrible message that the prophet has been proclaiming for the Holy One. So, it is a matter to be resolved between Jeremiah and the God of Israel, the God whose mission has turned Jeremiah's friends against him. The section ends with the most poignant prayer in the whole Bible, a cry in which Jeremiah accuses God of sending him on a self-destructive mission and then, like Job, wishes that he had never been born (Jer. 20:7–18).

Between the first confession and the last, the book's editors lead the readers through a hardening of the command not to intercede for the people, a command that had already been delivered in Jeremiah 11:14. In the context of the awful drought described in chapter 14, the prohibition becomes a heavy burden for the prophet. But there are also astounding statements of hope for the nations in Jeremiah 12:14–17, and again in Jeremiah 16:19–21, which open the horizons a bit and allow the action to continue. As we might expect, there are several terrible descriptions of the disasters that the Holy One will inflict on the people of Israel because of their wickedness (Jer. 13:1–27; 15:5–9). Symbolic actions are ordered by the Holy One in Jeremiah 13:1–14 and 19:1–15, actions designed to dramatize for the prophet and the people the destructive intentions of their God. And in Jeremiah 16:1–13 we have a personal prohibition barring Jeremiah from forming a family.

In sum, this long section reflects on the impossible alienation of the Holy One from Israel after the covenant has been suspended. There is a lot of personal pathos in the presentation of Jeremiah in these chapters, which have some of the most compelling material in the whole Bible. We should not imagine, however, that the fate of the prophet is the primary concern of scripture here or anywhere. The scriptures are about the history of a relationship between God and God's people. The word of God is an essential element in this history, and the prophet is the bearer of that word. The prophet's fate is simply a result of his mission of proclaiming the word of God when that word has become a declaration of death and exile. There can be no happy ending for such a people and no satisfactory ministry for a prophet in such a situation. The prophet is a victim of a situation much bigger than he, and these chapters explore that situation by focusing on the figure of the prophet.

We should not assume that the Jeremiah we encounter in the book of Jeremiah is the "historical" Jeremiah, the man who lived in the last decades of Judah's existence and experienced the destruction of Jerusalem and Judah. The Jeremiah tradition transmits materials that come at least in part from the prophet, but Jeremiah's successors, the editors, use the figure of the prophet to reflect on the fate of the people. So, when in this commentary I speak of Jeremiah, I usually mean the literary figure given us by the successors of the prophet. One often suspects the presence of a real, living person, especially in the prayers, but we can never be sure, and there is no reason to make the power of the scriptures dependent on their reflection of the historical person of Jeremiah. We must be content with the literary persona the tradition has given us. This Jeremiah has a great deal to say to we who live in the wake of the Gulag Archipelago, Hiroshima and Nagasaki, the Shoah, the bombings of Dresden and Baghdad, the war against the people of Vietnam (who were caught in the middle of a conflict between imperial powers), and other aspects of the awful legacy left to us by the twentieth century. Accounts have been written about prophets of our own whose fate was not too different from that of Jeremiah: Mahatma Gandhi, Dietrich Bonhoeffer, Martin Luther King Jr., Ernesto "Che" Guevara, the "crazy" mothers of the Plaza de Mayo, Nelson Mandela, and Archbishop Oscar Arnulfo Romero.

Expect hostility, prophet! (Jeremiah 11:18—12:6). God has just revealed to Jeremiah that the covenant of the Holy One with Israel is broken because Israel has failed to listen. The prophet has been instructed to deliver this message to the nation (Jer. 11:1–17). Jeremiah 11:18—20:18 draws out the consequences of this message, focusing on the figure of the prophet as the bearer of the brunt of his people's anger. The section begins with two prayers in which the prophet addresses the God who has sent him on his tragic mission (Jer. 11:18–23 and Jer. 12:1–6). These prayers are built on the lament model, common in the book of Psalms. As in most laments, we see three dramatic personae: the supplicant, God, and the enemy of the supplicant. Jeremiah's laments are, however, more personalized than those we find in the Psalms, because the enemy is named as "the men of Anathoth" (Jer. 11:23) or "your kinsfolk and your own family" (Jer. 12:6, NRSV). Because of his terrible message, the prophet has become the enemy of his own family!

The structure of the first prayer is quite straightforward. It begins with description of the calamity (11:18–19): Jeremiah is being led to slaughter like an innocent lamb. The speaker then praises the Holy One's righteousness (11:20), expressing assurance that the prophet's lawsuit (*riv*) will result in vengeance on his enemies. The surprise comes in God's response (11:21–23). The fact that God responds with an oracle within the psalm is not unusual, but the information communicated in this one is: God reveals that the enemies are people from Jeremiah's home town of Anathoth who are plotting his murder. However, the Holy One will indeed complete vengeance on them for Jeremiah.

The second prayer is rather different, although again structured as a lament, with the same three dramatic persons as most laments –supplicant, God, enemies. It opens with praise for the Holy One's righteous judgment, expressing the confidence that Jeremiah's lawsuit (again, *riv*) will find satisfaction from the heavenly judge (12:1a). But the psalmist faces a serious problem, that the wicked deceivers are rewarded even though they have God on their lips but far from their "kidneys," which were thought of as the seat of conscience (12:1b-2). (The kidneys are the location of the most secret thoughts and intentions of humans: Pss 7:10; 16:17; 26:2; Job 16:13.) The supplicant asks for vindication, confident that if God examines him he will be found upright (12:3). Further description of the trouble includes the accusation, frequent in the Psalms, that the enemies do not believe that God sees what they do (12:4). What we have here is the confrontation within the psalmist of two contradictory realities, his or her confidence that God is a righteous judge and the evidence on the ground to the contrary. Faced with these counter evidences the psalmist might give up and denounce God as a tyrant who does not care about justice. But "Jeremiah" refuses to take this course. He will maintain his trust in a righteous God, confident – or perhaps only hopeful—that the wicked will receive their just deserts. God's answer (12:5-6) is not very sympathetic to Jeremiah's plight: He must expect further difficulties and hostility from his own family. Implicitly, the expectation is that this is the role of the prophet, to provoke hostility. He must learn to trust nobody but God! But for his own sanity he must not let go of his trust in God.

These two prayers introduce the theme of the next chapters. These chapters, gathering poetic and prose materials about the coming judgment on Jerusalem and Judah, call our attention to the bind in which this puts the prophet. He is no longer permitted to pray for his beloved family and people nor even to call forthrightly for their repentance. He has become a Cassandra, a predictor of calamities, and like the Trojan Cassandra he must know that his predictions will bring upon him the hostility of his family and people. The truth of the predictions will only be known after the event. Until then, the prophet will seem like a pessimist or, worse, a traitor who does not wish well for his own people.

Again, we see that the prophet's role is not the role of pastor or priest. From a pastor or priest, we expect counsel and comfort. Jeremiah is neither a counselor nor a comforter! He is called to blow the whistle on the evils of his time and to sound an alarm about the tragic consequences to come. But the moment does not seem tragic to his contemporaries, so the sharpness of the whistle grates on their ears, and the alarm seems merely alarmist. He unsettles the people and becomes unwelcome. Archbishop Oscar Arnulfo Romero used his weekly homilies, which were broadcast on Catholic Radio in San Salvador, to inform people in the cities of the atrocities the army was doing in their name to poor people in the countryside. He warned them of the calamity that they, the government and the army, were bringing on the nation. He called for rank-and-file soldiers to disobey their superiors' orders and to cease killing innocent people. Bumper stickers appeared with the message, "Haga patria, mate a un cura" (Build the fatherland, kill a priest). On March 24, 1980, Romero was killed by a sharpshooter as he led mass in a hospital chapel.

The point is that in times of moral crisis the prophet must proclaim a message that appears to be treasonous. His murder then becomes a matter of patriotic duty that can even cancel the bonds of familial affection. The hostility Jeremiah faced in his home town had nothing personal about it; it was the protection of town and national interests and, as they saw it, also the protection of proper religion. The same can be said about Romero, or Martin Luther King Jr., or Gandhi.

Soliloquy of a wounded God (Jeremiah 12:7–13). This is a remarkable poem, as the poet creates the inner thoughts of the Holy One who has been forced to decide the destruction of the people God loves. As Hosea put it, "My heart is turned around, my innards are shaken" (Hos. 11:8). The Holy One is grieving in this remarkable poem at the sad state of God's beloved. Abraham Joshua Heschel, the great Jewish theologian, spoke of the sympathy of the prophets, their sharing the passions of God.[2] He argued that in the Bible it is more appropriate to speak of "anthropopathy" than anthropomorphism, because God is understood to have passions like those of humans. This poem is surely a magnificent illustration of how a prophet feels the feelings of God.

The Holy One does not deny a personal responsibility for the fate of Israel. The poem begins, "I have abandoned my house." It is God who invites the beasts of the field to "devour" Israel (Jer. 12:9). The poem closes with the sword of the Holy One "devouring" from one end of the land to the other (12:12). No proud and arrogant empire here, just beasts of the field who, without any conscious decision, devour the people whom God has put in their path. The destruction of Israel is the doing of the Holy One. It is not easy for the Holy One, because the object of these terrible actions is "the beloved of my soul" (12:7). We are reminded of the expression of the Song of Solomon, where the Shulammite seeks "him whom my soul loves" (Song 3:3,4). In the Jeremiah poem, however, the reference is less to desire than to grief over the loved one now lost forever. The prophet reveals here the tender side of the same Holy One who has unflinchingly rejected Israel for not listening to the messengers, who were sent without ceasing to turn her back to the correct path. Jeremiah is not saying anything new but reflecting poetically on the classic statement of faith from the Torah:

> The Holy One, the Holy One, merciful and compassionate, slow to anger and great in love and fidelity, showing love to thousands, who forgives iniquity, rebellion and sin, but does not leave them unpunished, who visits the sins of the ancestors on the children and children's children to the third and fourth generation. (Ex. 34:6–7)

The nations offered a new beginning (Jeremiah 12:14–17). In a surprising turn, this brief text offers forgiveness and a new beginning to the nations who taught Israel to worship the Baals, if those nations will learn "the ways of my people"! The whole text, which is more prose than poetry, is addressed to "the wicked neighbors" in the land the Holy One gave to Israel. The "ways of my people" are evidently the ways that people ought to have followed and not the ones they actually followed. The way of Israel back to the Holy One was closed firmly in Jeremiah 11:1–17, but now it is opened to the nations who provoked Israel's apostasy! These "nations" may be Israelites living in dispersion among the nations (over against those still in the land). Whoever they are, any people that does not "listen" will be uprooted and destroyed (12:17).

God is indeed beyond human fathoming! The Bible summarizes it all in the amazing and contradictory statement quoted from Exodus just above, about a God merciful and loving but also relentless with sinning peoples to whom God's servants the prophets have been sent. In a reflective mood, the writer of Ecclesiastes says, "Do not haste with your mouth or let your heart speed to issue a word before God, for God is in heaven and you are on earth; therefore, let your words be few!" (Eccl. 5:2; in Hebrew, 5:1).

Muslims open every prayer with the opening line of the Qur'an: "In the name of God, the Clement, the Merciful." Neither the Qur'an nor the Christian Bible take this first and last word about God to be the only word. If this were all there was to say, we would hardly require prophets to speak the cutting word of the living God. The editors put this little piece here to remind us, the readers, of the unfathomable mystery of the love of God, who is the same God who does not leave sins unrequited. What can we say? A mystery indeed!

The Holy One instructs Jeremiah (Jeremiah 13:1–14). These two scenes are centered on two symbols, a linen sash and a wine bottle. They resemble symbolic actions of the sort that are abundant in Ezekiel and of which there are some in Jeremiah. But there is no report in either of these texts of the delivery of a message to the people of Judah, just instructions to the prophet regarding the message he is to deliver.

The text concerning the sash (13:1–11) instructs Jeremiah to buy a sash, to wear it without washing, and then to take it to the Euphrates and hide it under some rocks. After a time, he is instructed to return and dig up the sash, which will be rotten and useless. The Holy One compares the destruction of the sash to the destruction that the Holy One is planning on the pride of Jerusalem, because they have not "listened to" (obeyed) God's word.

The sash sequence is intended as an object lesson to the prophet, but it is not evident how he is to interpret it. A clue is given in verse 11, where the closeness of the sash to the flesh is compared to how the Holy One drew the people close to Godself. It seems, then, that the prophet is to consider how while the people remained close to God things went well (the sash held up), but when they separated themselves from God, they were spoiled. The image is imperfect, for the sash is taken away by its wearer and hidden while the people deliberately abandoned God in spite of God's purposes for them. But the idea of closeness/health, separation/destruction makes sense and may help the prophet understand his message.

Evidently this text is really intended for the reader more than for Jeremiah. It is hard to believe that the prophet could have made two trips to the Euphrates, which might have taken a month each, first to deposit the sash and then to recover it. The mention of the Euphrates is the first allusion to the Babylonian exile that will play an important role in later chapters. Babylon has not yet been mentioned in Jeremiah up to this point. Aside from the significance of this allusion, it is difficult to see the point of traveling in order to bury the sash, which could have been buried in a field outside of Anathoth with the same result.

The conversation between the Holy One and Jeremiah about the wine bottle (13:12–14) is supposed to lead to a message of the prophet to the religious and political "Establishment" of Judah—kings, priests, prophets—and populace. But there is no report of the delivery of this message, as one would expect in a prophetic symbolic action. Like the linen sash, this conversation also anticipates what is to come later in Jeremiah, the drunken banquet of the kings of the nations in Jeremiah 25:14–29. "Before" that dreadful banquet, the leaders of Judahite society will become drunk with the wrath of their God because they failed to listen to God's word.

If, in the first symbol, judgment is presented as separation from God, in this symbol it is a drunken separation from reality provoked by the wrath of God. In our learning of godliness, or spirituality, as it is called today, the images are valid. Separation from God leads to self-destruction, like the sash that is taken off the body and left buried in the ground. In clinging to God, we can find our salvation. But it is also true that a separation from God leads to a loss of reality like that experienced in a drunken stupor. To bow down to the idol of wealth and endless consumption can lead to a state in which we no longer recognize loss of community and in which participation in imperial adventures appears realistic to protect our false world. So, it appears that the Holy One's lesson for Jeremiah is really a lesson in spirituality for the readers of this remarkable book of the Bible.

Lady Jerusalem to be publicly shamed (Jeremiah 13:15–27). Following the private instructions to Jeremiah come three poems directed to Jerusalem and its rulers. Verses 15–17 are a poem that reflects the pathetic tears of the prophet over the fate of his people and a plaintive plea for repentance. The prophet is aware, because God has just told him, that repentance is not possible for this people, but still he appeals for sense. The dominant theme is one of light and darkness. Give God glory while you may still expect light for your feet, before darkness sets in! Failure to respond will surely lead to irreparable darkness. Because he knows that the darkness is coming, the poet ends this piece with his own tears over his people. There is a resemblance between this poem and the divine soliloquy we read in Jeremiah 12:7–13 where God poured out grief over the destruction of Israel.

The brief poem in 13:18–19 is phrased as message from the Holy One to Jeremiah for the king and the queen mother. This is not a call to repentance but rather an appeal for them to lament the destruction of the cities of their kingdom. The cities are closed up and the population has been deported. Royalty must step down and sit on the ground in keeping with the awful fate of the people under their care.

This poem should be understood as an anticipation of deportation and not a reflection on the already accomplished fact of deportation. The prophet *knows* what is not yet evident to the rulers nor to the people. They are still living in the delusion of normalcy, confident in *sheqer*, an appearance that is not worthy of trust (13:25). How difficult it is for rulers to truly *see* reality behind appearances, when it is the world of appearances that has put them in power! In our time, one remembers the courage of Pope John XXIII, who called the Roman Catholic Church to look at itself as the world saw it and to shape up to reality. Perhaps one should include among these reality-perceiving rulers Frederick DeKlerk, who initiated negotiations with Nelson Mandela, a political prisoner with absolutely no power, who nevertheless represented reality in South Africa of the early 1990s. More often, the prophet is a voice calling in the wilderness, and although he or she may call in poetic appeals for the rulers to face reality, there is little or no hope for positive response.

The climactic poem in this little collection is in 13:20–27, a menacing address to Lady Jerusalem. Her shame is to be publicly exposed. She does not perceive the troops approaching from the north (13:20). Can she not tell that pains like those of birth are setting in? But it is not birth that provokes these pains (13:21). The scenes of shaming nudity that follow are predicated on the impossibility of repentance, a repentance that is like asking Ethiopians to change the color of their skin or the leopard to be rid of its spots (13:23). Verses 22 and 26 speak of the public exposure of the genitals of this refined Lady, whose adulteries and prostitutions will be publicly known (13:27). This disgrace, rather than the delusions of grandeur by which the "Holy City" lives, is true reality.

Prophetic poets are most unpleasant people to have in the midst of any society. But they are the barometers that pick up the pressures of reality that we ordinary persons in the doings of our daily rounds fail to detect. Typically, the prophet is quite out of sync with his or her society. Jeremiah is presented in drilling repetition as such a one. Typically, the prophet ends up in martyrdom, murdered, jailed, or submitted to public ridicule. Moses was publicly abused. Jesus was crucified. Yitzhak Rabin was assassinated, as were Malcolm X and Martin Luther King Jr. Yet, how necessary prophets are if a society is to be in touch with reality, to see itself as it is seen by the rest of the world! May God always give us prophets with the fire and the literary gifts of Jeremiah!

Stop praying for this people! (Jeremiah 14:1—15:4). In Jeremiah 11:14, the Holy One instructed Jeremiah not to pray for his people. They had not listened to the demands of the covenant, and neither would the Holy One listen to their supplications. Placed where it is, the text we are now looking at is a last attempt by the prophet to bear the burdens of his people before their God. The Holy One decisively refuses to listen. The door is slammed shut on any petitions for this people!

Much of this text is in the form of lament/petition, a prayer form familiar from the Book of Psalms. Jeremiah 14:1–9 and 14:17–22 are in lament form. Jeremiah 14:10–16 and 15:1–4 fit into these laments in the places where one would expect an oracle of salvation in response to the psalmist's petition. These are in fact a sort of response by God, but it is a response that closes the door on any future response and reaffirms judgment for this people.

Jeremiah 14:1–6, a lament over drought, has an introduction that speaks of a word of the Holy One, but instead of an oracle of God we find a description of calamities suitable to a psalm of lament. The situation is dramatic. Youths, sent to the springs to search for water, return with empty jars (14:3). Those who till the soil cover their heads in grief at the impossibility of getting anything out of the dust (14:4). The hart, that peaceful creature of the fields, brings forth her young and abandons it for lack of pasture (14:5). The wild ass stands on the hills and gasps for air, its eyes bulging because of the lack of grass. We should probably understand this not as a description of a factual drought but as the result of poetic imagination. The prophet looks around at the life in Judah, bustling about as if there were no problem, and sees a drought where there is and can be no life. The drought is the reality behind the appearances in Judah.

Verses 7–9 are the petition section traditional in all laments. The bases for the petition, the motives to get a response from God, begin with a confession of the guilt that justifies the disgrace. We have sinned, and our fathers committed apostasy (14:7). In the following lines (14:8–9), a striking accusation is directed at God for indifference in the face of the people's plight. The Hope and Salvation of Israel behaves like a foreigner passing through the land, who beds down for the night but has no commitment to the land. The appeal to God's honor in the next lines is a traditional motivation to get some action from God to defend God's name. Why are you acting like a warrior who is unable to save? Your Name is named over us. Do not abandon us! Jeremiah is praying, in spite of God's orders to refrain from doing so!

In the lament form, we would next expect an oracle of salvation promising deliverance to the petitioner. Instead, in Jeremiah 14:10–16, the Holy One tells God's prophet to tell "this people" that God will come to punish them for their wanderings (14:10). And there is more: God addresses the prophet to order him to cease praying for this people. Prayers and fastings and hymns are all useless. The decision to execute judgment has been made, and the door is closed.

Jeremiah is not content to leave it at that. In verse 13, he informs God that the prophets of Israel are promising good things and assuring the people that no ill will befall them. Again, the Holy One brings up the question of falsehood and reality: The prophets are dealing in *sheqer*, lies, delusions. God has not sent them, so their messages are not reflection of the reality that is God. They shall die in the judgment, along with their wives, sons, and daughters. Who can fail to be taken aback by the parallels to our time? Most ministers of religion are assuring their people that all is well and that failings in our world are relatively minor and external, some drug trafficking and terrorism that can be dealt with by military force. When millions of children are suffering from undernourishment, and the AIDS plague is forcing a rapid drop in average life expectancy in much of the world, to mention only a couple of the symptoms of reality, can we still speak a word from God that is not a call to repentance and action to relieve the death that abounds in today's world? We face a reality crisis, and most ministers of religion are dealing in *sheqer*, which is today the ingenuous faith that the Market will one day solve all these problems. And we, Christians, are often oblivious to our share in the guilt for a world gone awry. Nevertheless, the problem is not ascribing guilt, but facing reality, and our religion ought to help us do so.

In Jeremiah 14:17–18, someone—the prophet? God?—cries for the people. The speaker is probably the prophet, who goes out to find distress everywhere and cannot contain the tears in his eyes, but it could be God. In any case, one thing that he finds is the priests and prophets wandering aimlessly about, still knowing nothing. The reality defect of the official representatives of God, the religious Establishment, is part of the tragedy of Israel's destruction at the hands of God.

In spite of the slammed door, Jeremiah continues to appeal for his people in verses 19–22. Is it possible, he asks God, that your soul finds Zion abhorrent? The mention of Zion reminds us that the dominant theology of the time was temple theology and that the Jerusalem temple, by then the only "legitimate" place of sacrifice, was the king's chapel where royal ceremonials were held and prayers for royalty were part of the liturgy— Westminster Abbey, so to speak. Zion theology assured its adherents that the Holy One had chosen Zion for a dwelling (see Ps. 132) and had chosen David and his line in perpetuity as God's instrument (see 2 Sam. 7). In the official religion, it was unthinkable that the Holy One should abandon the people God had chosen as God's very own. "We," therefore, expected peace and restoration of health and find none. The plea leads up to a reminder of the Holy One's covenant with Israel (Jer. 14:21), which the Holy One has already said is no longer in effect.

The final appeal is a contrast between the true religion of Israel and the false cults of the other nations. We do not believe that the *hevalim* of the nations can bring rain or can restore health, says Jeremiah (14:22), because it was you, the Holy One, who made all things. *Hevel* (plural *hevalim*) literally means vapor. It is the favorite word of the writer of Ecclesiastes: "*Hevel* of *hevalim*, all things are *hevel*," (Eccl. 1:2; 12:8). For that writer, it often means something like foul stench. When used for the false gods of the nations, it means something like vanity, like the mist of the morning that dissipates when the sun burns hot. The petition asks, isn't true religion worth something? We know the truth and know that salvation, that is, rain, can only come from the Holy One who made the heavens.

God responds in Jeremiah 15:1–4 to the petitioners for whom the prophet has spoken. God answers with a round and absolute negative. If the door was slammed in Jeremiah 14:12, it is now opened just enough to be able to slam it harder than before! Even if you should be able to raise Moses and Samuel, great men of prayer, I would not listen, says the Holy One. Tell them, says the Holy One to the prophet, should they ask where they are to go in this situation, that death lies ahead in one form or another. This is reality!

Once again, an oracle of judgment (Jeremiah 15:5–9). We have already heard that Judah and Jerusalem are at the end of the road, about to be destroyed by the Holy One. Now, a fresh oracle conveys the same message in new images of death. The Holy One addresses Lady Jerusalem in the second person feminine singular. She must expect to be abandoned by all, including her God, who is tired of compassion! Widows shall be multiplied, and the one who bore seven, usually an honored one, will be drained of soul and disgraced. Coming after the prohibition on praying, this is a confirmation of the judgment given with the breaking of the covenant in chapter 11.

A prayerful conversation between God and Jeremiah (Jeremiah 15:10–21). This is another of the intimate prayers that are known as the confessions of Jeremiah, strategically placed in the large collection we are examining (11:18—20:18). In its context, one notes a marked difference between the way the Holy One deals with the sins of Israel and God's dealings with the sins of Jeremiah.

Like the other prayers in Jeremiah, this one can be understood as a lament, a genre very frequent in the book of Psalms. Jeremiah begins by addressing the Holy One to describe his situation of disgrace, which is a result of his prophetic ministry (Jer. 15:10–11). We have heard about the enemies of his own family who tried to kill him (Jer. 11:18—12:6). Here, Jeremiah reminds God that he always prayed for them (a statement that may not seem quite honest to the reader who remembers that Jeremiah asked God to avenge him, 11:20). God's first response, in Jeremiah 15:12–14, is not addressed to the prophet at all but is a restatement of the condemnation of Israel, addressed to the people of Israel. Jeremiah takes up his cause again, asking for vengeance against those who persecute him (15:15–18). In the description of his situation, the prophet affirms that his calamitous isolation from family and friends is directly caused by his role as God's prophet of doom. He reminds God that he, the prophet, has received bitter words with joy and devoured them like sweets. But God has been for Jeremiah a deceptive brook, whose waters are not reliable. We are reminded of the poet's image of an Israel that has exchanged living waters for cisterns that cannot hold water (Jer. 2:13), except that now the prophet accuses the Holy One of being deceptive waters for him, God's prophet.

The divine word in this lament comes, as one expects, at the end (15:19–21). It is a challenge to Jeremiah to shape up, to stop whining, and to take heart in the assurance that, with God on his side, he need not fear from his enemies. God will make him a bronze wall against which they shall fight but shall be unable to prevail (15:20).

Have no children and no social life! (Jeremiah 16:1–13). Jeremiah has many terrible passages, but this is one of the most awful. Because the judgment of the Holy One has been determined for the people of Israel, Jeremiah is ordered to cease normal social life immediately. If Israel knew what was coming, they would also refrain. No funerals, no weddings, no celebrations of any kind. The children who are born now will die terrible deaths, and their bodies will be eaten in the fields by the beasts with no one to mourn them. It is a terrible prospect, all because the ancestors abandoned the Holy One, and the present generation, God says, has been worse than the ancestors in ignoring the word of God.

The passage begins with an instruction by the Holy One to the prophet not to get married and have children, with the emphasis on the prohibition against having children. But already in Jeremiah 16:3, it is apparent that this is not so much about the prophet as about the fate of any children born at this time in Israel. The word of God for the people of Judah is not to have any children, so as not to increase the pain of the destruction that is imminent.

In the early twentieth century (1918), a German prophet of woe, Oswald Spengler, wrote a book he called *The Decline of the West* (Der Untergang des Abendlandes). One of the most important signs of decline, according to Spengler, was the drop in the birth rate in Europe and the United States. A people content not to raise children or to have only one is a people who no longer are able to affirm life. Probably, Spengler was right about the significance of the dropping birth rate in the "developed" nations of the world, where even today one finds a reluctance among young people to have children. The issue is not simple, as is shown by the case of China, a planned economy where vigilance to prevent the birth of too many children is public policy. Is this a case of a death wish on the part of the rulers who set the social patterns in that great country? Everywhere, East and West, though perhaps not yet in the South, there seems to be a resignation to the inability to sustain life for all and, hence, a general feeling that the numbers of new humans should be restricted to the social capacity to sustain them. Is this a failure of the will to life, as Spengler believed? Perhaps so.

But in Jeremiah the case is different. The Holy One, the same God who ordered the first humans created to "be fruitful and multiply," now orders the prophet to abstain from having children because it is not a time for life but for death. Children should not be brought into the world to die terrible deaths, which is what would happen should Jeremiah and his generation continue having children. In the rabbinic discussions recorded in the Talmud, the order to have children is considered the first of God's commands and one that requires strict obedience, so much so that a man devoted to the study of Torah who fails to fulfil his procreative duties is said to know the Law but to fail to do the Law. It is indeed a major catastrophe when the Holy One, the creator of life, orders a cessation of the production of new life!

And yet, there is hope! (Jeremiah 16:14–21). The latter part of chapter 16 presents a surprising reversal of the hopeless and antisocial perspective of Jeremiah 16:1–13. Here we have three texts, two that seem to be prose (16:14–15 and 16:16–18) and a final one in verse (16:19–21). The overall tone is hope, for even though the middle piece is judgmental, its location between two oracles of hope relativizes its judgment. These three pieces, or at least the first and the third, are surely late additions of the Jeremiah tradition, composed by successors of the prophet who believed that the judgment he had announced was fulfilled, and the time had come for hope. Yet, the texts are substantially the same in LXX and MT, which means that even the first edition of Jeremiah to which we have access had already affirmed restoration after the exile. At any rate, in our Bibles, judgment and hope lie side by side. The hope does not cancel the judgment but must somehow take it up into itself. It is as in the New Testament, where the resurrection of Jesus Christ does not cancel his crucifixion. Rather, the hope of resurrection passes through the agony and the defeat of Calvary. There is, in Christian scripture, and there can be, no resurrection without death, and, in the case of the Messiah, no triumph over the tyrant Pontius Pilate without going through the defeat of the legal assassination of Good Friday.

The prose in Jeremiah 16:14–15 is reminiscent of Isa. 43:16–21, a lovely poem that says virtually the same thing as our text (in more elegant language). Perhaps the transmitters of the Isaiah traditions and those of the Jeremiah traditions were in contact with each other.

The poem in Jeremiah 16:19–21 is a surprising promise that the nations who worshipped idols will recognize the folly of their ways and turn to the Holy One. They shall confess the *sheqer* of the ways of their fathers, whose *hevel* cannot save (16:19). This poem thus repeats the message of the prose piece in Jeremiah 12:14–15, a minor theme in the book but one whose presence is significant.

The oracle about the fishers and the hunters (16:16–18) does not identify their victims, though the mention of "my land" strongly suggests that it is the people of Judah who shall be fished and hunted. The placement of the oracle after the promise to Judah and before the promise to the nations introduces some ambivalence, which is no doubt intentional. Restoration can only follow judgment for peoples who have sinned.

The wise man and the fool (Jeremiah 17:1–11). The poem about the apostasies written on Judah's heart with a diamond-tipped chisel (Jer. 17:1–4) confirms the judgment the Holy One has issued. Coming as it does after the prediction that the nations will repent of their idols (Jer. 16:19–21), it is doubly damning of impenitent Judah. The whole poem is omitted in the earlier version of Jeremiah preserved in the LXX, which makes it likely that it was added exactly at this location to underline the contrast between impenitent Judah and the repenting nations (or scattered, exiled Israelites?). (The chapter divisions were made in the Middle Ages, so originally 16:19–21 and 17:1–4 were not separated as they are in modern Bibles.)

Verses 5–11 contain two poetic reflections very much in the style of Israel's wisdom teachers. Verses 5–8 mark out the contrast between the evil end of the fool, who trusts only in humans, and the prosperity that can be expected by the wise one, who trusts only in the Holy One. They are like two trees, one planted in the desert and the other by running waters, with the result we would expect. The image is familiar to Bible readers from the psalm that was put at the head of the Psalter by its editors (Ps. 1).

Verses 9–11 reflect on the Holy One's ability to penetrate the human heart and God's readiness to give each person the deserts of his or her actions. If one should attempt to steal what is not one's own, like the partridge that sits on an egg she did not lay, one will soon be bereft of the ill-gotten gain and be shown for what he or she is, a fool (*nabal*). That God examines heart (in Hebrew, the seat of thinking and decision as well as feeling) and kidneys (in Hebrew, the seat of deep emotions, usually concealed, and conscience) is a familiar idea to readers of the Psalms and Proverbs, though the image of the partridge is not. Still, the message of a God who watches over all to keep order in creation is familiar.

Why should these wisdom sayings be placed in the book of Jeremiah by his successors? Placed as they are after a series of devastating pronouncements of judgment and orders not to plead for Judah, one reads them as "philosophical" reflections to assure the reader that the Holy One is not an arbitrary tyrant who delights in punishing the people Israel that God has chosen. The biblical God is certainly problematic, sometimes merciful and pardoning and sometimes holding sins to account until the third and the fourth generations. Unless the ordinary Israelite and the ordinary Christian today can believe that, in the end, God is just and that, in spite of frequent appearances, God rules the world with justice, religion is pointless. An arbitrary God is worse than no God at all. The writer of Ecclesiastes cannot see justice in the everyday expressions of the rule of God in a world that stinks (is all *hevel*), but even he recommends that his disciples learn to enjoy their work (Eccl. 3:13), keep the faith (Eccl. 5:1–7; in Hebrew, 4:17—5:6) and enjoy the small pleasures of life, food, drink, and companionship (Eccl. 9:7–10). The false god of Wealth is today's *hevel*, a beautiful but useless cloud that does have more power over the lives of supposed believers than the religious and communal requirement to rest and enjoy life together.

Praise to a God of judgment (Jeremiah 17:12–13). This is a little hymn inserted between the wisdom poem we just looked at, which reflected in the abstract on the fate of the just person and the evil one (17:1–11), and Jeremiah's prayer for vindication against his adversaries (17:14–18). In the overall context of chapters 11 to 20, judgment is dominant, and this hymn is thus appropriate. The "throne of glory" is the place of sanctuary (17:12), a reference it seems to the Jerusalem temple. The speakers are the people of Israel ("our" sanctuary).

But as it turns out, the presence of the throne of glory is no defense for a wicked people of the sort that Jeremiah has been denouncing. Those who abandon God will be put to shame by the "hope of Israel" (17:13a). In verse 13b, God Godself speaks up to deal with those who abandon God, that is, the persons just mentioned in verse 13a. What they have done is to abandon the source of running water with the consequences of drought elaborated in Jeremiah 14 and referred to in Jeremiah 17:6. It is an obvious truism, well known to the sages, that without water life cannot subsist in the land. The reference to "running" water is a reminder of Jeremiah 2:13, the accusation that by abandoning the Holy One, Israel has exchanged a source of running water for cisterns that are cracked and cannot hold water.

In sum, this little poem is a hymnic reminder in wisdom style of the consequences of having a God of judgment in the midst of Israel. Surrounded by judgment poems, it is more a threat than a source of hope.

Heal me! Hasten judgment on my adversaries! (Jeremiah 17:14–18). Again, we have a prayer of Jeremiah. And again, it is modeled on the psalms of petition or lament in the book of Psalms. This prayer opens and closes with petitions (17:14 and 17:17–18) that enclose the description of the plight of the supplicant (17:15–16).

In an expression of confidence ("you are my prayer"), the supplicant, who is clearly the prophet of the other prayers in Jeremiah, asks for restoration of health (17:14). As the prophet moves into description of his calamity, the reader is again reminded of the adversaries who accuse and even threaten the life of the prophet (17:15). This is a common situation in psalms of lament, and the prayers in Jeremiah help show how those psalms were perceived as relevant to pious Israelites, who in real life suffered from enemies who pursued them. In Jeremiah's case, the enemies mock him for preaching a message of disaster in a time of peace. "Where is the word of the Holy One? Let it come" (17:15). From the passages we have been reading, we can see this is a fair description of the prophet's predicament, and we shall see more still to come. Verse 16 presents a problem, since it reveals the prophet as less than honest with the Holy One. The prophet claims not to have wished a day of distress for his adversaries, but this does not hold up in the light of the wishes he expressed in Jeremiah 12:3 and 15:15. Nor does it match Jeremiah 17:18 coming up, where the prophet urges God to bring the day of evil (the day of the Lord) on his adversaries. Israelite supplicants do not have hang-ups about wishing evil on their adversaries, to judge by a prayer like Psalm 109 and similar curses in other psalms. Jeremiah shows in verse 16 a brief misgiving about these desires for the judgment of his foes—but he gets over it quickly.

We have seen in the former prayers, as in many psalms of supplication, that God answers. That is, the prayers include oracles of salvation. This time, Jeremiah gets no answer. God has told his people through the prophet not to bother praying, and it seems that this applies also to the prophet. Judgment has been determined, and it is useless to pray. A frightening thought!

Keep my Sabbaths and you shall prosper! (Jeremiah 17:19–27). This text is surprisingly hopeful, considering Jeremiah's insistence on the finality of the Holy One's decision to declare the covenant with Israel suspended. If they stop bearing burdens in and out of the gates of Jerusalem on the Sabbath, the people of Jerusalem shall see prosperity. If the people sanctify the Sabbath, then kings, chariots, horsemen, and other signs of wealth and power will pass through the gates that are now polluted by the practice of moving merchandise on the Sabbath.

The Sabbath was one of the central demands of the Holy One's covenant with Israel. It was one of the Ten Commandments issued by the Holy One directly to the people on Mount Sinai. The Sabbath was sanctified by ceasing all forms of work. Not only was the Israelite to stop working, but also the Israelite's son, daughter, manservant and maidservant, ox and ass, and the foreigner who dwelt in his city (Ex. 20:8–11). The Sabbath was to be a sign of the covenant, a practical matter that distinguished the people of Israel from the other nations of the world. Its observance was the strictest law:

> Keep the Sabbath because it shall be holy for you. Anyone who profanes it shall die. Anyone who does work during it shall be wiped out from the midst of his people. Six days you shall work, but the seventh day shall be a day of total rest, sanctified to the Holy One. Anyone who works on the Sabbath shall die. The people of Israel shall keep the Sabbath from generation to generation as a perpetual covenant. It shall be a perpetual sign between me and the people of Israel, for in six days the Holy One made the heavens and the earth, and on the seventh day God ceased and restored God's spirit. (Ex. 31:14–17)

Numbers 28:9–10 prescribes special Sabbath offerings in addition to the daily offerings, and Lev. 23:3 even speaks of solemn assemblies on the Sabbath, but these were not essential. The special thing about the Sabbath was always the required rest for all Israelites, for their beasts, and for their workers. This was the sign of the covenant with the Holy One.

The Sabbath rest was also an *Imitatio Dei*, a way in which the believer could be holy as God is holy, doing himself or herself what the Holy One did after six days of creative labors at the beginning of time (Gen. 2:1–3).

In very early Christian circles, the communities, at that time made up mostly of Jewish people, began observing as "the Lord's Day" the first day of the week, because on that day Jesus Christ was raised from the dead. Already in the book of the Revelation to John, there is evidence of this practice (Rev. 1:9–10). Up until the twentieth century, it was a nearly universal practice among Christians to cease their labors and to give rest to their workers on Sunday, the first day of the week. For Christians, it was also a day of worship, of gathering to praise God, firstly for the creation and the resurrection, and also to hear the preaching of the word of God. Christians, besides worship, often sought out forms of recreation on Sunday that did not require the labor of others, things like walks, rides in the country, or visits to the beach. By their respect for the Lord's Day, believers were bonded together and singled out among populations that did not necessarily observe rest or gather for praise that day.

Karl Marx thought that the only true God of his time was Capital, that is, money or merchandise that seeks to make more value. Practice in our times would seem to prove him right. On the day Christians used to call the Lord's Day, one can find Christians working in stores, gasoline stations, and restaurants, and others using the labors of people who work in such centers. Owners of these establishments feel the "need" to keep them open on Sunday because, in contemporary Christian societies, it is a good business day. The need is, of course, the "need" to make more money even if it means weakening the fabric that draws society together around its common godly practices. The God these Christians praise in church is less important to them than the God they serve in their businesses.

It is this flaunting of one's disregard for God and community that Jeremiah—I remind the reader that this Jeremiah is the persona in the book and not necessarily the historical Jeremiah—finds objectionable in his people. In the name of the Holy One, he promises prosperity for Jerusalem, a very rare promise in his book, should it repent and keep the Sabbath as the Holy One ordained it to be kept. It should give us pause that this most severe prophet, who usually demands a generalized obedience to the word of the Holy One, makes a promise of blessing conditional on the keeping of the Sabbath rest.

The lesson of pottery: No change is possible any more! (Jeremiah 18:1–12). After toying with hope in the section just finished, the lesson in the potter's shop is a return to the message of certain damnation for Judah.

The Holy One orders the prophet to go to the potter's shop and watch him work. During the formation of the pot on the wheel, adjustments can be made in the shape that the pot will eventually assume. On this basis, lessons are drawn about God's alternative courses of action in God's dealings with nations. This section of the matter is drawn out at some length in order to stress the openness of God in dealing with nations.

Curiously, the first instance has to do with the plan of God to uproot and destroy a nation. Should that nation desist from its evil course and return to the ways of God, God will "repent" from the evil planned for that nation and send it good fortune. Conversely, if God should plan good for a nation and that nation should turn away from God's instruction into evil paths, God will "repent" of the good intended for it and will uproot and destroy it. The book of Jonah illustrates perfectly this openness of God in God's dealings with the nations—in Jonah's case, with the evil empire Assyria. When Nineveh repents upon hearing Jonah's preaching, the Holy One repents (or has a change of mind) of the evil God had determined to send them (Jon. 3:10), with the same verb for repentance used in our text, a verb usually applied to humans, but in these two texts (and also in Ex. 32:14; 1 Sam. 15:11, 35; Amos 7:3, 6) used of God's repentance. Our Jeremiah text is an unusual "philosophical" reflection on the way God acts, or rather interacts, with the nations. In the section we are examining (Jer. 11:18—20:18), there has been a quiet presentation of God's dealings with "other" nations (Jer. 12:14–17; 16:19–21), of which this text makes generalizations. However, the message of this passage is for Israel, which explains the priority of the negative plans of the Holy One over the positive plans, when we would expect positive ones in the light of the example of the potter's work.

The conclusion, beginning with *ve'attah*, "and now" (18:11–12), is no longer a generalized reflection but directed straight at Israel. The time for invitations to repent is past. Israel has assumed a hardened position and will not repent. Although not made explicit in the text, the idea seems to be that the clay has been fired and can no longer sustain alterations. The plans of the Holy One for the destruction of Judah and Jerusalem will no longer be altered, not because the Holy One cannot alter plans but because the people have hardened beyond change (like the pot that has already been fired).

In this way, as we approach the end of this section, the verdict on the rupture of the covenant in chapter 11 is reaffirmed and sustained.

An unheard-of change for the worse (Jeremiah 18:13–17). Here, the editors have inserted a poem of judgment to accentuate the firm determination that came out of the visit to the potter's workshop. The point of the poem is the amazement that any nation should exchange the Holy

One for "nothing" (*shav*). There is always snow on the heights of Lebanon, and there is always water in running streams, but, incredibly, Israel has turned away from the Holy One, from secure highways to unknown paths.

Violent reaction to the word of God, and Jeremiah's response (Jeremiah 18:18–23). In Jeremiah 18:19–23, we find another of the prayers of Jeremiah, this one, like the former ones, dominated by the mention of enemies who seek the prophet's death because of his message about a reality unknown to his compatriots. The editors have introduced it with a statement about the plot against Jeremiah's life. We are reminded of Jeremiah 11:18–23 and the plot by the men of Anathoth, though the enemies are not identified here. They are those who reject the destabilizing influence of Jeremiah's message. For them, as for most religious leaders anywhere and anytime, a prophet's message should be constructive. The reference to the instruction of the priest, the counsel of the wise, and the word of the prophet (18:18) refers to this religious consensus, which Jeremiah is breaking and defying. The prayer of Jeremiah follows in verses 19–23.

This prayer has little that is new, and it is basically a call for vengeance against enemies, a call already heard in Jeremiah 12:3 and, especially, 17:14–18. One feels in these last two prayers an intensification of the nonconformity of Jeremiah with the negative side to his calling, a nonconformity that he has expressed from the beginning of his prayers.

Breaking the pot and the priest's reaction (Jeremiah 19:1—20:6). In the first part of this narrative, 19:1–15, the pottery image continues. Now, Jeremiah is ordered to take a finished pot and carry it to the Valley of Ben Hinnom, south of Jerusalem, accompanied by representatives of the Establishment. He is ordered to deliver a terrible message of destruction, culminating in the breaking of the pot as a symbol for the irreparable damage that the Holy One is to bring on Jerusalem. Upon his return from the Valley of Ben Hinnom, he is to deliver his message of inevitable destruction in the temple precincts (19:14–15).

The place where he is to break the pot is evidently of significance. In this valley, there was a sanctuary of some sort where the burning of human children was practiced, a sacrifice that Jeremiah denounces as completely foreign to the commands of the Holy One (19:5). The fact that he must say so suggests that some people in Jerusalem believed that it was an order of their God, probably the command to offer the firstborn (Ex. 13:1–2, 11–16; 34:19–20; Num. 18:15). This is confirmed by the reference in Ezek. 20:25–26 to such a command of the Holy One for child sacrifice that was given only to test Israel. Surely, for those who practiced it, child sacrifice must have been perceived as the ultimate gift a man or woman could offer to God. During the conquest of the New World, Bartolomé de Las Casas argued that Indian human sacrifices were not murders but that the natives were offering the best they knew to God, ignoring that this was not what God desired (*Historia de las Indias,* written during the 1540s, though published later. In spite of its title, this work is really an anthropological study of the natives of the Indies and not a history. The argument about human sacrifice was probably used against Juan Ginés de Sepúlveda in the famous Valladolid disputations of 1552 on the justification of the wars against the natives of the Indies, a disputation held at the invitation of the king with the purpose of examining royal practice in its new colonies, a most remarkable event for an imperial power!). But if God is not pleased with this sacrifice, it becomes murder, and that seems to be one of the points Jeremiah is making here, when he says that Topheth shall no more be called Topheth or the Valley of Ben Hinnom but the Valley of Killings (19:6). This is a very serious accusation and must have been heard as a totally unacceptable prophecy by the established religious leaders whom Jeremiah invited to accompany him to the place where child sacrifice was offered. In Jeremiah's opinion the sacrifice was offered not to the Holy One but to Baal, another god (19:5). At issue then, is the question of true worship and the true God, always a very difficult one to adjudicate. Everyone who offers sacrifices does so because he or she believes it will be acceptable to the true God. So, the statement that the sacrifices are worship of Baal, the wrong god from Jeremiah's perspective, is an accusation of very serious self-deception, a costly self-deception that has led to the loss of believers' own children.

And for Jeremiah, the punishment fits the crime. The people of Jerusalem will be reduced by the war against the city to eating their own children (19:9). Topheth, according to MT, will become a cemetery, and there will not be room for all the bodies, which will be eaten by the birds of the heavens and the beasts of the fields (19:7, 11). LXX does not have the reference to burial at Topheth (19:11), so it should be understood as an addition, perhaps a softened explanation of the Valley of Killings in Jeremiah 19:6. However, LXX translates the word Topheth with a Greek word for cemetery (*polyandrion*) every time it appears in this chapter, so that it was understood by the translators that the Valley of Hinnom was, in fact, a place of burial.

This is a gruesome text, but it is language with a purpose, language designed to shock the listeners into recognizing that a reality they perceived as normal was in fact deadly. Modern prophets do similar things with their images, as when Marx accused the Europe of his day of worshipping Capital as the only real God and spoke of Capital as "dead labor" that sucked the blood of living workers. The factory became in Marx's analysis a place that manufactured death along with the merchandise. Living workers drew that merchandise out of machines that represented the dead labor of their predecessors. Their heavy work on these products of dead labor, the machines, sucked their life-blood from them. And there is, sadly, still today a lot of truth to the dramatic images that Marx used for the workplace.

Within the book of Jeremiah, this gruesome text wraps up and underlines the theme of covenant breaking that was announced in chapter 11 and repeated with many different images thereafter. Judah and Jerusalem can only expect, says Jeremiah in words the Holy One has given him, the worst sort of national death. There is a growing movement today that challenges the global economy as a factory of death. The outbreak of the Zapatista rebellion in the state of Chiapas was staged for January 1, 1994, to coincide with the initiation of the North American Free Trade Agreement (NAFTA) of Mexico with the United States and Canada. People were surprised at the massive protests in the streets of Seattle in November 1999 during the meeting of the World Trade Organization, protests that we have seen at other world economy meetings in Cologne, Quebec, Prague, Genoa, and Davos. It is evident that the "Free Market," which for the Establishment of our time is the solution to all the world's problems, is for many others the instrument of the deaths of multitudes of people who are excluded.

As a result of the prophecy that Jeremiah delivers to the representatives of the Establishment in the sanctuary of Topheth and in the courtyard of the temple, the priest in charge of keeping order in the Jerusalem temple has Jeremiah placed in some form of restraining device by the Benjamin gate of the temple (Jer. 20:1–6). The text before us is a personal oracle of judgment against this priest, a man named Pashhur. For the first time, the conquering empire, the identity of which was hinted at by the mention of the Euphrates in 13:7, is named and cited as the location of the coming exile. Its name is—no surprise for readers who know the history—Babylon. From here until the end of the book, Babylon is going to play a major role. Of course, Babylon was present from the beginning but hidden as "the enemy from the north." Now, the enemy has been named.

The judgment pronounced against Pashhur is exile. He will be taken to Babylon along with all the wealth he pretends to protect in Jerusalem, and he will die in Babylon and be buried in that land. With the privatization of life in Europe and the United States in our times, it is perhaps difficult to appreciate the terror of the collapse of one's community and one's own displacement to a foreign place. In other times and places, the loss of communal identity is a form of death while one still breathes and walks. For a person like Pashhur, with a high position, to be removed from the city where he is a grand personality would even today be a dreadful blow.

Think of what it means to a powerful senator to lose an election and have to return to his hometown as just an ordinary citizen, like those he claimed to represent.

It is not clear why Pashhur's example should be a terror more than any other figure being taken away into exile. Perhaps it is that he holds a powerful post, and it is terrifying to see him reduced to a stranger in a foreign land, one who will depend on small favors he may be able to get from his captors—or, perhaps he will not even be granted small favors. He no longer will command the power to put anyone in stocks or to prevent his captors from doing this to him, should they wish to do so. Perhaps it is the greatness of his fall that will make it terrifying to all around him.

The prophet overpowered by God (Jeremiah 20:7–18). Without a doubt, this is the most impressive of Jeremiah's prayers. With this prayer, the editors bring to a close the section on God, Judah, and the prophet (Jer. 11:18—20:18). This portion of the book opened with a prayer of Jeremiah, who was faced with a murder attempt from his family, and now closes with another prayer of Jeremiah, struggling hopelessly against a God who overpowers him. Power is the key to this prayer. "You were able" (*tukal,* that is, had the power, 20:7). "I was not able" (*lo' 'ukal,* 20:9). "We shall be able against him" (*nuklah lo,* 20:10). "They shall not be able" (*lo' yukalu,* 20:11). "My days end in disgrace" (*vayyiklu bebosheth yamay,* 20:18, here with a play on the verbs *yikklu,* "shall end," and the various forms of the verb *yakol,* "to have the power, to be able").

Jeremiah begins his prayer with a cry of protest over the violence with which God has forced him into a hopeless situation, where he must announce violence all the time and become the object of violent plots against his life from his erstwhile friends and family. The suggestion of Jeremiah 20:7 is that God has "raped" Jeremiah. In this awful situation, Jeremiah attempted to be silent, but he was unable, that is, did not have the power, to contain the fire in his bones. This description of the trouble of the supplicant/prophet in Jeremiah 20:7–9 presents the powerlessness of the prophet in the face of the irresistible power of God. No human enemies yet appear on the scene, but God Godself is an enemy, as well as a judge who must listen to Jeremiah's case (*riv,* lawsuit, 20:12).

Verses 10–13 are a traditional lament in which the prophet expresses confidence in God's righteous judgment, which will free him from his enemies who will not be able to carry out their violent plans against him. But evidently, the real problem is not the enemies who make fun of him and seek his life. Jeremiah's real problem is God, who has called him to an impossible task. The prayer ends in verses 14–18 with curses on the day of his birth. Jeremiah wishes that he had died in his mother's womb and not seen the days of shame that his life as a prophet has brought him.

This is a powerful statement, one of the jewels of the Bible's spirituality! We are told several times in the Bible that a human cannot see God and expect to survive (Ex. 33:20; Deut 5:24–26; Judg. 6:22–23; Isa. 6:5). The rabbis advised that extreme precautions must be taken even in speaking of God's chariot in the vision of Ezekiel 1. But here we have a poet/prophet, a person of great spiritual sensitivity, describing the terrible experience of encountering the Holy One. In liberal Protestant preaching and theology, God often becomes a sentimental, kindly, old father who would do no harm to a flea. This is not the God of the Bible. The God of the Bible reserves the right to exercise vengeance on the enemies of God or of God's people (Lev. 19:18; Deut. 32:35; Ps. 94:1; Rom. 12:19). We have seen, in Jeremiah's prayers, his confidence in the vengeance God will take on his (Jeremiah's) enemies. In the early church, this issue was raised by Marcion, a theologian from Pontus on the Black Sea, who came to Rome between 130 and 140 C.E. He excised the Hebrew scriptures from his Christian Bible because he found in them a violent God. In response, Tertullian, an African theologian of about 200 C.E., wrote five long and vehement books *Against Marcion,* in which he demonstrated that neither Jesus nor Paul believed that God could not or would not exercise judgment on evil persons. It is a dangerous matter to take the living God seriously and attempt to follow God's demands. Many persons have been killed for doing so. Many more have gotten into serious trouble. In times of crisis, as ours arguably is, the person who takes God seriously is separated from the crowd and may end up struggling with God as Jeremiah did, in prayers that show that both love and hate.

Conflicts with Kings, Prophets, and Nonexiles
(Jeremiah 21—24)

We are now approaching the center of the ring structure in the MT version of Jeremiah (see pp. 3–4). Jeremiah was announced in Jeremiah 1:5 as a prophet to the nations. Now, the prophet confronts the kings of Judah and the other nations with the Holy One's word. The words are ones of judgment.

This section presents a series of judgments, to be followed by chapter 25, which is the center of the MT edition of the book. A second series of judgments, parallel to those in Jeremiah 21—24, follows in 26—29.

F. Conflicts with kings, prophets, and nonexiles

    F1. Conflicts with the monarchy of Judah (21:1 and 23:8)

    F2. Conflicts with the false prophets (23:9–40)

    F3. Conflicts with those left after the deportation (24)

        X. Sentences on Judah and the nations

            X1. Sentences on Judah and Jerusalem (25:1–14)

            X2. Sentences on the nations (25:15–38)

F'. Conflicts with kings, prophets, and exiles

    F'1. Conflicts with the monarchy of Judah (26 and 27)

    F'2. Conflicts with the prophets (28)

    F'3. Conflicts with those deported (29)

Prophet Confronts King During Siege of Jerusalem
(Jeremiah 21:1–10)

Zedekiah, the king of Judah, surprisingly sends a high-level delegation of Pashhur and Zephaniah to consult Jeremiah in search of a word from the Holy One. The forces of the empire are at the gates of Jerusalem, and military defense is not sufficient. All resources must be mobilized, including the search for God's word. Interestingly, and not surprisingly, the nations today that most oppose the impositions of empire are those who gain their confidence from their obedience to God, nations like Iran and Libya that openly embrace Islam (whose name means obedience) and officially practice God's law (the *Shari'a*). In the strength of God, they feel empowered to challenge the vastly superior might of the U.S. empire, which they realize they cannot successfully oppose on purely military grounds. In the case of Zedekiah's Judah, the situation is different, because Zedekiah does not resort to the Holy One until his other resources are exhausted. But he does turn to God at the last, by means of the prophet Jeremiah.

Interestingly, Zedekiah knows the language of salvation. His message is: "Perhaps the Holy One will act for us according to his wonders (*nifle'otav*) and will make him [Nebuchadnezzar, the Babylonian king, whose name is often spelled "Nebuchadrezzar" in the book of Jeremiah] withdraw from us" (21:2). The *nifla'ot* would include the exodus and all its wonders of divine might, well known in Israelite lore and frequently recited in the liturgies of Passover. The king knows that such wonders are all that can save him. This is, no doubt, the feeling of some in Iran, Libya, and other small nations of the world when they face down the United States.

The prophet answers, in effect, that the Holy One is now fighting on the side of empire against the city of Jerusalem. The Chaldeans are outside the walls. God will gather them to the center of the city. It is the Holy One who will fight the dwellers of this city with "mighty hand and outstretched arm" (a phrase familiar from such Torah passages as Ex. 6:6 and Deut 4:34; 5:15; 7:19; 9:29; 26:8). There will be "plague, sword, and hunger" (21:7) for the dwellers of Jerusalem. Zedekiah and his servants, who will survive the siege and final battle because of their privileged places and their access to food stocks, will be captured by the king of Babylon and taken to Babylon as exiles. Empires do not tolerate resistance to their designs, and Nebuchadnezzar will show no mercy.

Jeremiah also has an unsolicited word, this one for the people of Jerusalem (21:8–9). They face a choice between "the way of life and the way of death"—language familiar from Moses' farewell speech to Israel on the plains of Moab (especially, Deut. 30:15–20). According to Deuteronomy, loyalty to the Holy One is the way of life and acknowledgment of foreign sovereigns is the way of death. But now, says Jeremiah, the way of life is to leave the city and surrender to the Babylonians; staying in the Holy One's city is the way of death by "plague, hunger and sword." For Jeremiah to propose this to the people, including, of course, the young men in the army, is high treason in the eyes of the authorities.

It is hard, oh so hard, to resist the crowd in times of collective enthusiasm for "national defense." German pastors like Martin Niemoller and Dietrich Bonhoeffer showed great bravery in standing against the patriotic fervor of the German people in a time of war. Just when the nation called upon everyone to put every ounce of energy into the war effort, these pastors/prophets stood up and said, "this mighty regime is not worth supporting; we resist in the name of Jesus Christ." Secular scientists like Albert Einstein and Leo Oppenheimer showed similar bravery when they unsuccessfully resisted the military apparatus's efforts to develop an atomic bomb. Their resistance was not popular at a time when the war effort against the Axis seemed to justify all means, however costly in civilian lives. The editors of the book of Jeremiah present the prophet to us as a man willing to defy his people's war effort in the name of God. The lesson for ministers of religion today is clear: Be brave! Let your faith, nourished by your religious traditions and your direct experience with God, give you the foundation for taking distance from the powers that govern your country (and the world)!

Do Justice, Free the Oppressed! (Jeremiah 21:11–14)

The poem or poems that end this chapter are directed to "the House of David," in other words to the whole of the government across the generations. God is going to judge them according to the justice they executed or did not execute and by their readiness to intervene when the poor were being oppressed by the stronger. This is an excellent measuring rod for any government of any country, rich or poor, at any time. It will be applied to individual kings of Judah in the next chapter, but its relevance extends far beyond them. How does the U.S. government rate by this measuring rod? Franklin D. Roosevelt's social protections, especially Social Security, have been chipped away, as have the measures from Lyndon B. Johnson's War on Poverty in the 1960s. The United States is just about the only rich country in today's world without a universal health care program (a situation from which private health insurance companies profit greatly). The United States has housing programs for the indigent, but these programs are usually contracted to private construction companies. In general, the U.S. government, alone among the wealthy nations in today's world, does not assume responsibility for the survival of the poor even within its own borders.

Line 21:14a of this text, "when I visit them I will judge them according to the fruits of their deeds, says the Holy One," does not appear in the LXX. This line was added by the MT's editors to underline the general measuring rod in Jeremiah 21:11. Religious leaders today should take heed.

Judgments on the Kings of Judah (Jeremiah 22:1–23:8)

General judgment on the "house of the kings of Judah" (Jeremiah 22:1–9). Before listing and judging individual kings, Jeremiah offers an overall judgment on the recent kings of the Davidic line by the measuring rod he has just established. The result is devastating! The measuring rod is that the kings are to act with justice and righteousness (*mishpat utsedaqah*), to deliver the oppressed from the oppressor and to do no wrong to the poor, the widow, the orphan, and the stranger.

As we apply this measuring stick to our governments today, what stands out is the poor treatment given to the stranger, the immigrant. European cities such as Berlin discriminate against ethnic minorities such as Turks. The U.S. border with Mexico is heavily militarized, precisely to keep out the Mexican stranger who seeks to escape poverty. The United States calls itself "land of the free" but has no intention of extending its freedoms to the illegal immigrants it so zealously ferrets out. Only a tiny handful of churches show any awareness that the Bible might call for protection of such strangers.

Jeremiah is not the only biblical book mentioning God's preferential option for "the widow, the orphan, and the stranger" (see, for instance, Deut. 16:11; 24:19–21; Job 24:3–4; Ps. 68:6; 94:5; Isa. 1:17; 10:2; Mal. 3:5). Deuteronomy, in particular, emphasizes care for the stranger. But the concern appears in other books as well. Widows and orphans are relatively well cared for today, but governments have yet to come to terms with their responsibility for the stranger, even and especially in the face of hostility against strangers on the part of the population. As Christians, we believe God establishes rulers to punish evildoers—whether or not they are citizens—and to reward the good on the same basis (Rom. 13:4). In the Hebrew Bible, the resident stranger gets privileged treatment, along with the widow and the orphan. According to Jeremiah, kings have the special duty to give that privilege—even at times against general opinion, we might add, at a time when strangers are feared as potential terrorists even before they give any indications this might be so.

The reference to abandoning the Holy One for other gods in Jeremiah 22:8–9 may surprise us, since previous verses have emphasized injustices to the oppressed, the widow, the orphan, and the stranger. It reintroduces themes we saw earlier in Jeremiah 10 and 11. But there is a logic to the juxtaposition of injustice to the poor and worship of false gods. Israel's Holy One demands justice as an element of worship, whereas the other gods have other demands. In my opinion, the original demand, "Thou shalt not worship other Gods beside me" (Ex. 20:3), reflects the struggle between the Holy One of the slaves and the exalted gods of Pharaoh. Pharaoh's gods legitimate his rule, as the gods of Canaan legitimate its kings, and in both case the gods' demands have little to do with defense of the poor. Even when there is in some Egyptian and Mesopotamian texts an expression of concern for the welfare of the poor, I know of no text that threatens rulers with punishment if they fail to care for them, as does Jeremiah. Because of the connection in the exodus experience between loyalty to the Holy One and the redemption of slaves, it is perfectly understandable that here, and in many other places in the Hebrew Bible, there is an equivalence between worshiping the Holy One exclusively and caring for the poor.

In our society today, the false god that is most seductive is Capital. Whereas the God of the Bible demands service to the needs of the poor, the growth of Capital requires that these needs be subordinated to those of the Almighty Market. The issue is illustrated with the debate over Social Security. Roosevelt believed that this program would move toward a system wherein the government would increasingly assume direct responsibility for citizens' needs, without taking into account the different amounts each had paid in taxes for Social Security. Under the demands of Capital, the movement has been in the opposite direction. Today, President Bush urges that individual accounts be turned over to private capital and that the "owners" of these accounts be able to invest them as they wish. The government, hence, washes its hands of responsibility for the poorest in our midst, at least as far as Social Security is concerned. This is submitting to the demands of the false god Capital rather than the demands of the God of the Bible. So, we see how the worship of false gods has its social cost in the U.S.A., as well as in Judah.

The word of God confronts the kings of Judah (Jeremiah 22:10–30). In this unit, several kings—two sons of Josiah and a grandson—are condemned one by one. It is clear that for the book of Jeremiah, God governs through prophets and the word more than through kings.

The first king, Shallum, is dealt with briefly in Jeremiah 22:10–12. Shallum took power upon the death of his father, Josiah, in 609 B.C.E. and reigned for only three months. Josiah, who died in battle with the king of Egypt, is highly regarded in the books of Kings and also in this chapter (contrast the negative evaluation of Josiah's reign in Jer. 3:6–10). His sons, however, receive no praise. Shallum was taken away and locked up in Hamath to the north of Israel (2 Kings 23:33). Jeremiah assures his listeners that the deported king will never return to "this land" again.

More significant was the reign of Jehoiakim (Jer. 22:13–19). He was another son of Josiah and reigned from 609 B.C.E. until 598. Jeremiah's poem on Jehoiakim is very significant, one of the most powerful statements about the knowledge of God in the whole Bible! The scene is set by reviewing this king's love for building palaces complete with cedar paneling, the finest finish available in his time (22:13–14). The luxury of these palaces is contrasted with the conditions of the workers whose labor was underpaid. The king has exploited his workers in order to build himself more elegant places to show off. "Are you a king because you compete in cedar?" (22:15).

The indictment contrasts Jehoiakim's eating and partying with his father's practice of righteousness and justice (*mishpat utsedaqah*). Josiah "judged the cause of the poor and needy" (22:16); evidently Jehoiakim did not. Look carefully at what verse 16 says: "He judged the cause of the poor and needy; then it was well. Is not this to know me? says the Holy One." It does not say, "because he knew me, he judged the cause of the poor and needy," nor "because he judged the cause of the poor and needy, he knew me." Rather, practice of mercy for the poor *is* knowledge of God. Hosea 4:1–2 makes the same point in negative form: "There is no faithfulness or loyalty, and *no knowledge of God* in the land. Swearing, lying, and murder, and stealing and adultery break out; bloodshed follows bloodshed." Here the lack of faithfulness and loyalty is the same as no knowledge of God. Similarly, "Israel cries to me, 'My God, we—Israel—know you!' Israel has spurned the good" (Hos. 8:2–3). Both Hosea and Jeremiah have the same striking message, but Jeremiah with its positive formulation is clearer. The practice of mercy *is* knowledge of God. To try to substitute mere religious practices or beliefs for such justice/knowledge is self-deception.

The United States is the wealthiest nation in the world and, by most measuring sticks, one of the most religious. Attendance at religious services is much higher in the United States than in Japan or Europe. Belief in God is much more widespread than in China or Russia. But European countries almost all have universal health coverage, so residents can receive treatment for illnesses whether they have private health insurance or not. Laws to protect the rights of workers to organize are stricter than in the United

States. If we take these as measuring standards, one would have to say that the knowledge of God is greater in Europe than in the United States. But comparisons are pointless. By Jeremiah's standards, a country with very little health coverage for the poor and very weak labor laws, a country that has not signed most of the international conventions for the protection of workers or the environment, must be ranked low on knowledge of God, regardless of its citizens' religious beliefs and practices.

After an interlude on the cedars of Lebanon (Jer. 22:20–23), the text turns to Jehoiakim's son Coniah (22:24–30). This king is better known as Jehoiachin and also sometimes as Jeconiah. He inherited the crown from his father just three months before Babylonian troops arrived to reestablish Babylonian control over Judah. Along with many of his court, he was taken into exile in Babylon. Jeremiah's poem tells listeners and readers that Jehoiachin/Coniah will never again see the land where he was born. Nor will he have a son succeed him on the throne of David. These predictions were, in fact, fulfilled, although the prediction about the previous king's body, Jehoiakim, being dumped outside the city (Jer. 22:18–19) was not fulfilled (he had the good fortune of dying before the troops arrived and so was buried with the usual royal pomp and circumstance).

General judgment on the kings and promise of a messiah (Jeremiah 23:1–8). Having surveyed recent kings one by one and found them all short of God's requirements, the prophet now judges the Davidic kingship itself and finds it lacking. The shepherds have scattered rather than gathered the sheep. This being so, God will Godself do the saving deed that is required, to bring the people back from the various kingdoms to which they have been scattered. In that day, people in Israel will no more remember the exodus as their salvation but rather the gathering of the people from all the nations in which they have been dispersed (23:8).

In the LXX, the verses about the new confession (Jer. 23:7–8 in MT) appear after the oracles against the lying prophets (that is, they follow MT Jer. 23:40). This means that in the older edition of Jeremiah, the prophets were grouped with the kings as part of God's governance of Judah. By relocating the verses about the new confession, MT dramatizes the meaning of the return announced in Jeremiah 23:1–4 and also separates prophets from kings, as we separate politicians from ministers of religion today.

The passage goes on to promise that God will raise a "righteous Branch," a king who shall rule wisely and exercise justice and righteousness (*mishpat utsedaqah*) in the land. This "righteous Branch" is the eschatological king who will later be known as messiah. This is one of the clearest messianic texts in the prophetic books.

Jeremiah's judgment on kingship itself, rather than just individual kings, is the equivalent of challenging the U.S. governmental system rather than just individual presidents and secretaries of state. This goes farther than U.S. citizens usually expect religious criticisms to go. When "democracy" is preached in Third World nations, the U.S. is often presented as a model. But is a system in which successful national campaigns can only be carried out by those with access to very large amounts of money really an ideal model? And what about the exclusion of organized workers from the decisions that affect them in the work place? In addition, the usual hypocrisy of the United States when it comes to assessing human welfare is galling to much of the rest of the world. When annual reports on human rights are rendered to the U.S. Congress by a commission established for that purpose, all nations on earth are evaluated except one. Why not also make a critical examination of human rights violations in the United States?

The Prophets Who Do Not Proclaim the Word of the Holy One (Jeremiah 23:9–40)

The editors of the book of Jeremiah have pulled together in this section a collection of sayings that have to do with Jeremiah's prophetic rivals. It is evident that, in those fateful days in which Jeremiah lived, there were very different perceptions of what was happening and what the Holy One meant to do. Jeremiah had a small band of supporters: In later sections of the book we shall hear about Baruch, Ahikam, Micaiah, Shephetiah, Ebed-Melech, and others. Most of them were scribes, functionaries in the administrative apparatus of the kings of Jerusalem. But most of the religious representatives, the prophets and the priests, were rivals of Jeremiah. They had a very different perception of reality than he did and even supported those who tried to put him away. But we are getting ahead of ourselves. This chapter is not about that problem. This chapter directly addresses the other prophets in Jerusalem and denounces them for telling dreams of their own invention rather than pronouncing the word of the Holy One.

There is a fundamental problem here. Jeremiah was canonized and his rivals are now long forgotten, and this is, no doubt, because his message of destruction and exile proved to be a right analysis of the situation. Evidently, his rivals were struggling to give hope in this difficult situation (they spoke *shalom*, peace and welfare, 23:17) while Jeremiah was announcing the very opposite, the imminent destruction of the city and exile of its inhabitants. For Jeremiah, "the anger of the Holy One will not turn back until he has executed and accomplished the intents of his mind" (23:20). If the other prophets had been in the council of God, according to Jeremiah, they would proclaim a message of judgment. When they preach peace and hope, they proclaim lies in the name of the Holy One (23:18, 26). If they had stood in the council of God and proclaimed the word of God, "they would have turned [my people] from their evil way" (23:22). The word of God is like fire or a sledgehammer that breaks rock (23:29). In the end, the dispute is theological: Is God a nearby God who can be tamed for our interests or is God a God far off? (23:23). (At this point, there is a curious reading in LXX, quite opposed to MT: "I am a near-by God, says the Holy One, and not a distant God." It is easier to imagine that the MT saying was softened to that of LXX than the reverse. Most likely, then, the MT preserves the more original version of this saying, which was eventually modified in the transmission of the Greek text.) Those prophets who always announce peace and forgiveness in the name of a loving God do not know the harsh side of the living God, who comes upon the sinners like a whirling tempest (23:19).

In any given generation, there will be prophets who speak contradictory messages because they have different understandings of God and/or of the situation of their people. Faithful believers must, of course, discern true speakers for God from liars who preach their own ideas as the word of God. Discernment is easy after the fact, but we live only once and cannot redo our lives with the benefit of hindsight. From afar, we must distinguish the action and demands of God whose word is fire or a sledgehammer.

Today, we see opposing representations of God in the debate about the human value of the globalization promoted by the G-8 nations. Meetings of those nations in Seattle, Cologne, Quebec, Davos, and Genoa have sparked alternative meetings that have drawn amazing crowds from all over the world to protest the "new world order" and its destruction of humans and their natural environment. The protestors say that representatives of the people must have the power to control life-threatening transnational corporations. Those who are religious among them proclaim that God is a God of life, who desires life for the poor and not their death nor the destruction of natural resources. At some of these international meetings, demonstrators have been confronted by police, who have protected the representatives of the major powers. Other religious leaders, like the Cardinal of Genoa, announce in God's name that we need to give more power to transnationals for the ultimate welfare of us all.

We may need transnationals to produce the complicated equipment of modern technology, but if God is as severe a God as Jeremiah believed, we cannot allow the transnationals to function without restrictions. Their claim to work for the good of all is a lie. The year 2000, proclaimed as a Jubilee year by the pope, passed with almost nothing cancelled on the enormous debts owed by poor countries to banks in New York, Tokyo, and Zurich.

Most of these odious debts were contracted without consulting or, in some cases, even informing the people of the nations involved. The loan money was spent by dictators in fashions that were never clear. The debts thus incurred require poor countries to export vast sums of capital to the rich banks of wealthy nations. The banks, major representatives of transnational financial enterprises, have done almost nothing to remove this illegitimate yoke from the necks of the world's poor people. How can they continue to claim that they bring prosperity, when the beneficiaries of that so-called prosperity are always an elite far removed from the people?

Nevertheless a majority of religious spokespersons in our world defend the global order, which sustains them with generous salaries, allowing them to live lives of leisure and to travel with their families around the world. Who speaks the word of God? Jeremiah had a firm and hard answer. Do we, the prophets of this time and age?

Exile of Jehoiachin and the Remnant of Zedekiah (Jeremiah 24:1–10)

In 597 B.C.E., the Babylonian king Nebuchadnezzar took control of Jerusalem, deported the young king Jehoiachin and other important leaders to Mesopotamia, and placed Jehoiachin's uncle, Zedekiah, on the throne. According to 2 Kings 24:14, Nebuchadnezzar carried away "all" from Jerusalem—all the officials, all the warriors, all the artisans and smiths, ten thousand captives, leaving only the poorest in the land. But according to Jeremiah 52:28, he took only 3,023 Judeans and in 586 B.C.E another 832 persons. Evidently, the book of Jeremiah assumes that the exile was less than total. In this, no doubt, it reflects historical reality. Even if the exile of 597 B.C.E. were the ten thousand claimed by Kings, that would have been less than the total of the population of Jerusalem, not counting that of other Judean cities like Lachish and Hebron.

After all we have heard from Jeremiah, his response to the deportations in 597 B.C.E is a surprising one, for it praises the exiles who went to Babylon with the young king Jehoiachin and condemns the remnant who were left in Jerusalem with Zedekiah. All this is tied to a vision of figs—also a little suprising, since Jeremiah's revelations normally come in oral form (unlike Ezekiel, who frequently reports visions). The Holy One shows Jeremiah two baskets of figs lying before the temple. One has good, juicy figs, and the other has figs so bad they cannot be eaten. The Holy One proceeds to interpret the vision. The good figs represent those who were taken to Babylon by Nebuchadnezzar along with Jehoiachin in 597 B.C.E. (24:4–7). The Holy One has plans for them. "They shall be my people and I will be their God" (24:7). This expression (also found in Jer. 7:23; 11:4; 30:22; 31:33; 32:38;

and in Ezekiel and elsewhere) is a powerful affirmation of divine election. Here, it is used with a surprising exclusivity to refer only to the Jehoiachin exiles! The Zedekiah remnant and the Egyptian exiles are explicitly excluded, compared by the Holy One to the figs of the second basket, so bad they cannot be eaten (24:8–10).

Thus, Jeremiah is invited by God to declare divine support for one group in distinction from others. This is surely a dangerous precedent! It is not just like saying God has a preferential option for the poor, including women, Native Americans, Africans, and similar groups of the poor. It is like saying that God opts for some poor over other poor, women before Africans or vice versa.

The passage becomes more understandable—although perhaps not any more palatable—if we remember that the book of Jeremiah was put together by the *golah*, the Judean exiles who returned from Babylon. They sharply distinguished themselves from the "the people of the land," poor peasants who cultivated the land and whose families had never gone into exile. They also distinguished themselves from the Judeans exiled to Egypt in 586 B.C.E. and those who went a few years later after the murder of Gedaliah (the governor appointed by the Babylonians), and even from the Judeans who were exiled to Babylon along with Zedekiah in 586 B.C.E. Jeremiah 24 reflects the concerns of the *golah* group in a time after 538 B.C.E., when Cyrus permitted them to return to Jerusalem. Within the ring structure of Jeremiah, this chapter corresponds to chapter 29, Jeremiah's letter to the exiles in which he urges patience but promises restoration in God's own time. There, too, Jeremiah is depicted as throwing his weight with the Jehoiachin exiles over the later Zedekiah exiles (29:16–19).

The presence of Jeremiah 24, which reflects this *golah* perspective, in both the LXX and MT shows that neither version can be ascribed in its present form to Jeremiah himself or to his scribe Baruch. Both LXX and MT have been shaped and expanded by much later editors. Yet, members of the returned *golah* accepted the book as Holy Scripture and Jeremiah as a model of prophecy. The willingness of this group to add to Jeremiah's work and to recognize the additions as authentically inspired legitimizes our own "rereadings" of Jeremiah for our own times. If Jeremiah could serve in the construction of a Judean community after the restoration, he can also serve in the creation of a postimperial society in the twenty-first century.

PART X

Sentences on Judah and the Nations
(Jeremiah 25)

When a book is organized in a ring structure, as Jeremiah MT is, its center receives special emphasis. We learn in the book's introductory vision that Jeremiah is to be a "prophet to the nations" (Jer. 1:5). Judah soon becomes the first of these nations (1:10–19). Jeremiah 25 devotes its first fourteen verses to the Holy One's judgment upon Jerusalem and Judah. The remainder of the chapter declares judgment on the rest of the nations. God calls Jeremiah to a task that goes beyond his own country. God's prophets today may well be similarly called to speak to the nations.

Jerusalem to Be Destroyed for Its Disobedience
(Jeremiah 25:1–14)

Jeremiah 25:1–14 is set in the fourth year of the reign of Jehoiakim, which was the first year of Nebuchadnezzar's reign in Babylon. This means we have moved backwards in time from the previous chapter, which was dated in the reign of Zedekiah, the second king after Jehoiakim. After messages to various kings (21:1—23:8), messages to the prophets of Judah (23:9–40), and the condemnation of those who were not exiled in the first deportation (24:1–10), Jeremiah 25:1–15 provides a global judgment on the city of Jerusalem and the nation Judah. Giving the date by both Judean (fourth year of Jehoiakim) and Babylonian (first year of Nebuchadnezzar) reckonings foreshadows the crucial role of Babylon in the Holy One's plan. (The LXX, which lacks MT's ring structure, does not mention Nebuchadnezzar or Babylon in Jer. 25:1. Babylon will still play a crucial role, but LXX delays revelation of that role until later in the book.)

Jeremiah begins his words to "the people of Judah and all the inhabitants of Jerusalem" with a reminder of his fruitless ministry. For twenty-three years, he has tirelessly ("getting up early," rendered in many English translations with terms such as "persistently" or "again and again") proclaimed the word of God, and "you have not listened" (25:3). Once again, we see the prophet pictured as a solitary figure who fights against the current. This is not a typical religious leader in either Judah or the contemporary U.S.A. Jeremiah's "colleagues," the other prophets, announce peace to his generation (Jer. 23:17). Preachers in our pulpits similarly assume the general rightness of contemporary society or they would lose their positions. From the vantage point of the *golah*, returning from Babylon to govern Judah with the support of the Persian authorities, Jeremiah was an attractive figure not because he turned against the stream but because he predicted both Babylon's dominance and its eventual downfall. Their grandfathers in Jehoiakim's day would surely have opposed Jeremiah, but hindsight gives them a new and "better" perspective, and that perspective has become canonical for us as Jews and Christians. Now that both the Babylonian and the Persian empires are past history, we see the prophet as a brave religious leader who saw through the wickedness of his generation's leaders and the population's docility to proclaim a dissident message of judgment. How important it is in an imperial power like the United States to have such dissident voices!

In hindsight, the prophet becomes one who offers forgiveness to those who repent of their evil ways (Jer. 25:5,6). This does not agree with statements in Jeremiah 11—15 forbidding the prophet to intercede for the people of Judah nor many other texts where judgment is proclaimed as a fact already determined in the heavenly court. But for the *golah*, the image of Jeremiah extending one last chance means that those now being excluded from the *golah* restoration project (Ezra 4) must deserve to be excluded. After all, they and their ancestors had the opportunity to repent and didn't take it!

For contemporary Jewish and Christian leaders in the United States, the presence of this offer of repentance and forgiveness has a different importance. We must offer our people forgiveness when they turn from evil ways. The future of the world is at stake! Unless the United States can repent and accept international treaties on disarmament, the defense of children and refugees, the protection of the natural environment, and labor laws that give organized labor a fair chance, there can be little hope for the world, given the wealth of the United States and its consequent influence on the rest of the world. The canonical Jeremiah can be a genuine role model for ministers of religion in the U.S.A. today.

With Jeremiah 25:9 we begin to see great differences between LXX and MT. In the LXX, verse 9 reads, "Behold, I am sending and I will bring a people from the north and lead them to this land and to its inhabitants and to all the nations round about and I will make them desolate and make them an object of horror and of hissing, and of eternal shame." The MT, reflecting a later stage in the book's development, identifies the enemy from the north with Babylon and Nebuchadnezzar as "my servant." This is a most remarkable theological affirmation: Is the merciless Nebuchadnezzar, who three times took Judeans into exile in Babylon, really an instrument in God's hand? We will shortly see God promising to punish Nebuchadnezzar for the delight and pride with which he carried out his mission, but according to Jeremiah and several other biblical books, the mission itself was given to the Babylonian king by the Holy One, the God of Israel! Empires may have their place in God's governance of the world, even when they are as ruthless as were the Babylonians. The expression "Nebuchadnezzar my servant" occurs three times in the MT edition of Jeremiah (25:9; 27:6; and 43:10), and in none of these cases is it in Jeremiah LXX. This must mean that this key theological reflection is a late one in the formation of the Jeremiah tradition. From this fact, we see the wisdom of the reflection of Martin Buber that the redactor (editor) is our rabbi (teacher), whose voice we must heed. Sometimes, the redactor has weakened the text, but in many cases, such as this one, the redactor has strengthened the text. For ministers of religion in an imperial country like the U.S.A., it is important to grant that, on occasion, empire can serve God's purposes, even when in the long run we must affirm that empire is not God's will for the governance of God's people. It cannot be the will of God that one nation should rule over others and become wealthy by sacking their riches. Such a nation will certainly fall in God's good time. Nevertheless, in the short run, which in some cases like the Roman empire may mean several centuries, God may have a purpose in the rule of empires.

The punishment of Babylon in MT Jeremiah 25:12 is, in Jeremiah LXX, a punishment of "that nation," unnamed. In this manner, the explicit mention of Babylon is put off yet a while (although the alert reader will already have spotted it in Jer. 20:5). But there would have been little doubt that Babylon was intended. As the saying goes in Spanish, "A todo chancho le llega su sábado" (To every pig his Saturday). No empire can last very long; of this we can be sure, even though we cannot be sure just when the day of the Lord will arrive. It is important that this obvious truth from history and our faith in a just God be made clear by religious leaders in the United States to their people. We must not imagine that the United States will be any different from Babylon, Persia, Greece, Rome, the Turks, and the many other empires that have flourished and perished under God's providence. Jeremiah 25:14, not found in LXX, summarizes what has been said in the previous verses.

The Cup of God's Wrath (Jeremiah 25:15–38)

Jeremiah is to take the cup of the Holy One's wrath and offer it in a horrific banquet to all the kings and nations of the earth, beginning with Egypt and ending with Babylon (25:26, Sheshak, a slightly veiled reference to Babel, see following p. 81), and between them passing through all the minor players in the panorama of Middle Eastern politics. When they drink of this cup, they will get drunk and vomit and fall to rise no more (25:27). They will be punished for their evil deeds with the sword that the Holy One is summoning against them (25:29).

How are we to understand this awful banquet? Jeremiah could not really have met with the kings of all the far-flung nations mentioned. No, Jeremiah really addresses the people of Judah with his word from the Holy One announcing the condemnation of all the nations of the earth. The message for Jeremiah's Judahite audience is that the Holy One, sovereign of all the nations of the earth, judges *all* of them for their sins. Judah will be judged first (25:1–14), but the process will extend even to the superpowers of Egypt and Babylon. Israel's sovereign God will not overlook Israel's sins, but neither will the Holy One leave the sins of the rest of the nations unpunished, for God is just and merciful, desiring Judah's ultimate salvation—and perhaps salvation for the other nations, also.

This chapter is reminiscent of Amos 1—2, except that Amos's oracles against the nations begin with other nations and end with Israel. Jeremiah reverses the order, but, in both cases, the most important target for the wrath is Israel-Judah. God's punishment begins (or, in Amos, culminates) with God's people, but both prophets wish to establish also that God will not leave the sins of any nation on earth unpunished. God is both able and willing to punish all for the evils they have committed, especially against God's people.

It is especially clear in this crucial chapter that the book of Jeremiah is the culmination of a fairly long process of traditions gathered and edited, then edited again before reaching the state represented by the MT and our modern translations. The comparison with LXX gives us a glimpse of this process. In LXX Jeremiah, the judgment on Judah (LXX Jer. 25:1–13) introduces a collection of oracles against the nations that the MT has moved to the end of the book (MT Jer. 46—51). After those oracles, in the LXX, comes the banquet with the cup of the wrath of God (LXX Jer. 32:15–38). In the MT, the six long chapters of oracles against the nations have been moved out of the center of the book and placed at the end, leaving the judgment against Judah and the banquet scene at the center of the rearranged book. In either arrangement, the judgment against the nations, with its affirmation of God's sovereignty over international politics, is very important to the book of Jeremiah. In the final edition, MT Jeremiah, the ring structure highlights the judgment on Judah (25:1–14) and the cup of wrath (25:15–38), with the collection of oracles against the nations at the end of the book counterbalancing Jeremiah's call in chapter 1:4–10. This neat arrangement may not be immediately obvious to the reader, but once it is spotted, the pattern highlights the new center of the book and underlines God's control over all of history, including the rise and fall of empires that in their peak seem to be invincible.

In the poem about the cup of the Holy One's wrath (MT 25:15–28), it is instructive to compare the earlier edition (LXX) with the last one (MT). We who are used to MT must remember that this scene is LXX Jeremiah 32:15–29 and not in chapter 25 as it is in MT. There are a couple of significant additions in MT, one in 25:18 and the other in 25:26 (these are not the only additions, but they are the most important). In MT Jeremiah 25:18, after the forecast of the ills that will befall Jerusalem and the cities of Judah, MT adds "as in this day," an indication of its perspective after the exile and the desolation of the land without its elite class. Jeremiah 25:26 ends, in the MT, with a reference to "the king of Sheshak" who will drink the final draught from the Holy One's cup of wrath. "Sheshak" is a thinly veiled allusion to Babylon, changing the letters in Babel to the comparable letters if one counts back from the end of the Hebrew alphabet (as if, in English, one substituted "z" for "a," "y" for "b," and so forth). This hints that the final edition was prepared after the fall of Babylon in 539 B.C.E. and so gloats over that fall. The fact that MT uses a cryptogram here, when it has just mentioned Babylon by name in 25:12, suggests that this dramatic "cup poem" circulated independently before it became part of the book of Jeremiah.

The poem is a powerful statement of God's control over history, even the histories of mighty empires. Empires always throw their weight around. Think of the arrogance of U.S. intervention in Bosnia, depending solely on its superior military might without any consultation of NATO, or how the United States drew up an artificial coalition of states and pressured the United Nations into supporting its war against Iraq in 1991. The situation of the second invasion of Iraq in 2003, against UN opposition, was also supported by a similarly artificial "coalition of the willing." One might think of the way in which disarmament treaties are being ignored by the United States as it insists on building an antimissile shield over the opposition of most other states in today's world. Might engenders the "need" to use it. Unless an army is used, it becomes rusty, so to speak. So nations such as Babylon, Rome, and the United States, each in turn, nations with a military capacity totally beyond any other in their times, feel compelled to find occasions to use that capacity, even when that means disregarding commitments they have made to less powerful nations. Religious leaders—prophets, priests, mullahs, professors of religion, rabbis, monks, pastors, and others—have an obligation to study and understand this dynamic and to guide their people in gaining a critical insight into the power movements of their day. As more Christians and other religious people understand what is going on, it will become harder for the generals and politicians to act on their first inclinations, that is, to find occasions to flex their military muscles

The God of Jeremiah 25 is a violent and wrathful God, a lion who has left his cave (25:38). This is the only kind of God who can deal with heavily armed empires and make him/herself respected. Believing in God the Creator means much more than believing in a God who set the scene for humans by providing plants and animals for nutrition and seas and rivers for travel and quenching thirst. A God who is Creator acts to influence the big movements of history, the rise and fall of nations and empires, small and large. We need not believe in an almighty God who acts arbitrarily according to divine desires. Such a belief is not confirmed by our experience of the world. But we must believe in a God who influences evolutionary processes from their earliest stages to the historical evolution of highly technological armies such as we see today in an empire like the U.S.A. This has gotten out of control, but if we believe in a Creator God, we believe that control will be restored, even if it means waiting for the long run, a scale beyond our short lives as human animals. We believe that God punished Nebuchadnezzar, as this poem from the Jeremiah tradition asserts, and we believe that God will put the military might of the U.S.A. in a place where it will no longer threaten world peace and the collective protection of the natural environment.

PART F'

Conflicts with Kings, Prophets, and Exiles
(Jeremiah 26—29)

These four chapters, Jeremiah 26—29 in our Bibles (and in MT Jeremiah), are a counterpart of chapters 21—24, dealing with Jeremiah's conflicts with kings, prophets, and exiled Judahites. But in this return to the same theme, there is a deepening of our understanding of the reasons for the conflict. These turn out to be profoundly theological or, if you prefer, ideological. Jeremiah, or at least the Jeremiah created by the postexilic community who wrote our book, represents a theology of uncompromising Torah loyalty. Those who obey the word of the Holy One and practice justice and the liberation of the oppressed can expect salvation for themselves and their people. Those who do not will just as surely be punished. In the book of Jeremiah, salvation means national freedom in the land given by the Holy One to the ancestors, and condemnation means submission to the empire and exile to Babylon.

Opposing Jeremiah are almost all of the kings, prophets, and people of Judah. They believe that God crowns the Judean king and is loyal to him, elects Jerusalem as a resting place and will defend it, and chooses a people and protects them in the land given to their ancestors. Such a theology is expressed in 2 Samuel 7 and Psalm 89. If the king disobeys, God may punish him but will not remove him or destroy him (see Ps. 89:28–37). As for the city, God chose Zion (a name used for Jerusalem in the context of its chosen status) for God's eternal dwelling (Ps. 132) and will always be loyal to the city. 2 Kings 18—19, 2 Chronicles 32, and Isaiah 36—37 tell of an instance in which God miraculously protected Jerusalem from Assyrian armies in the days of Hezekiah. It was probably this deliverance that Zedekiah had in mind when he said, in Jeremiah 21:2, "Please inquire of the Holy One on our behalf, for King Nebuchadrezzar [here, for Nebuchadnezzar] of Babylon is making war against us; perhaps the Holy One will perform a wonderful deed for us, as he has often done, and will make him withdraw from us."

The conflicts narrated in Jeremiah 26—29 are not just personal conflicts between Jeremiah and certain kings, prophets, and sages, but an encounter between two profoundly antagonistic theological perspectives. Is Israel's God the God whose unconditional promises to David cannot fail, or the God of Moses, who issues laws for a people and demands that they protect their holiness and their salvation by obeying the laws and listening to the word proclaimed by the Holy One's prophets? Jeremiah's answer, like that of Hosea and Micah, is diametrically opposed to the answer of the royal establishment in palace and temple. In Jeremiah 26—29, we see the conflict between mutually exclusive theologies that have both found a place in our Bible.

As we enter the twenty-first century, unless I am mistaken (which is always possible, of course), we are similarly engaged in a deep and irreconcilable conflict between opposing groups. This conflict has been dramatized for us at meetings of international organizations that defend the world market and its various expressions. The first conflict, which surprised the world, was carried out in Seattle in November 1999 during the meeting of the WTO. Similar conflicts took place in Cologne in 2000 at the meeting of the G-8 (the eight economically most powerful nations and their leaders), in Davos at the meeting of economic experts in January 2001, and at other meetings we occasionally hear about in our news reports. Increasingly police force is used to break up the protests and protect the meetings of the "big ones." But during the Davos 2001 meetings, an alternative meeting of economists, politicians, and journalists, several thousand strong, was going on in Porto Alegre, Brazil, to protest the Davos meeting and pose alternatives without allowing police forces to portray the protestors as "hooligans."

It is increasingly evident that we are not looking on a conflict between the defenders of social order and anarchists or hooligans who would create disorder for the joy of it. What we have is the clash of alternative views of the world order. The experts gathered at Davos each January and the people who gather at meetings of the WTO and IMF in various venues are defending an old world order where loans must be repaid and investments, foreign or national, must be protected, even if it means that whole nations (even most of a continent, in the case of Africa) are condemned to die of hunger and/or AIDS. The protestors in Seattle and the thousands who gather each January in Porto Alegre, in a city and state governed by socialists, are calling for a different world social order (order, not anarchy!) where the needs of people are given priority over the profit of those who invest large amounts of capital. They are studying how this can be done in a way that will not stop technological development, destroy the environment, or create vast pockets of poverty. They say it is better to experiment with the unknown than to allow a system that is destroying humankind to continue its devastating work. They don't want their proposals to be discarded as a police problem at meetings of the present world order, so they gather at the same time in the month of January but in a different location, Porto Alegre and, in 2004, in Mumbai, India.

Here we are faced with a dramatic clash not different in principle from the one faced by Jeremiah, though, of course, played out on a much larger scale. Increasingly, all of us are going to have to face a choice between these irreconcilable forces that are clashing on a global scale in our time. Perhaps there will be something to learn from Jeremiah and his opponents.

Kings, Prophets, and Priests Try to Kill Jeremiah (Jeremiah 26)

We have the first of several conflicts here in this chapter. The occasion is the Temple Sermon, apparently the one laid out in Jeremiah 7, although only the brief calls to repentance are quoted here. The date is the beginning of the reign of Jehoiakim, early in Jeremiah's career and long before the incident with Zedekiah mentioned in Jeremiah 21 (for a review of the kings mentioned in Jeremiah, see pp. 70–72). We see, then, that in the book of Jeremiah the ordering principle is not chronological. Instead, the conflicts in chapters 26 and 27 are counterposed to the oracles against the kings of Judah in 21:1—23:8. In Jeremiah 26, the king stands in the background, being publicly represented by his officials. Jeremiah's opponents are "the priests, the prophets, and all the people [who] heard Jeremiah speaking these words in the house of the Holy One" (26:7). Evidently, the religious establishment of Judah and its followers find Jeremiah sacrilegious or treasonous or both. They call for his death. When they report Jeremiah's words to the "officials," they say, "he has prophesied against this city" (26:11). They do not report Jeremiah's call to repentance.

Jeremiah's response (26:12–15), apparently addressed to everybody, repeats the call to repentance. Jeremiah says that he is willing to be killed, but this would just add the murder of an innocent man to the evil deeds already committed. Jeremiah is fulfilling the mission committed to him by the Holy One; the message is not his own but God's. Here we have God's representatives on both sides of a conflict, not unlike the situation we face today. Michel Camdessus, former director of the IMF, frequently interpreted its work as a case of the preferential option for the poor. He is now a functionary at the Vatican. But among the protestors at Seattle and at the meetings in Porto Alegre, there has also been a fair representation of ministers and theologians. One of the sites of class struggle is without a doubt the church, and theological conflict is often a reflection of the fundamental conflict of values we are discussing. What do the king's officials have to say in the face of the death sentence proclaimed by the religious representatives of Judah? It is a most interesting response! Jeremiah has a right to speak the word he believes to come from God and does not deserve death for doing so (26:16). No comment on the word itself, the call to repentance! But this rather timid, bureaucratic response emboldens a new sector of the population, the village elders, to speak up (Jer. 26:17–19). They recall the precedent of Micah of Moresheth, who said more or less the same thing about the destiny of Jerusalem and whose message was heeded by Hezekiah and the people at his time. Here is at least an implicit call to respond to Jeremiah's message with repentance. The conflict is then resolved—or at least deferred—when Ahikam, one of the sons of a distinguished scribe named Shaphan, takes Jeremiah away and puts him under his own protection. But there has been no repentance! Jeremiah's life is saved, but the larger issue his preaching exposed has been sidestepped. It would be tragic should this be the way in which the present conflict is "resolved," but it is perfectly conceivable, maybe even predictable, that the representatives of an alternative to the Global Markets will be given forums to speak and then be ignored.

Jeremiah against the Prophets of Judah and the Nations (Jeremiah 27—28)

These two chapters are joined by the theme of Jeremiah's conflict with the prophets. In Jeremiah 27, the prophet battles kings and prophets in general, not just those of Judah but of the nations, while in Jeremiah 28, he confronts one prophet in particular, Hananiah. These chapters, therefore, counterbalance Jeremiah 21:1—23:8, directed against the kings, and 23:9–40, directed against prophets who give messages without being sent by the Holy One. Jeremiah says they declare lies (*sheqer*, 27:10), so we tend to think of them as "false prophets," and so they are called in LXX Jeremiah (LXX Jer. 34:7, *pseudoprophetai*). But the Hebrew text calls them simply "prophets," and that reminds us that they were recognized prophets in Judahite society. They appear false to Jeremiah only because he operates from a fundamentally different theology. The same is true today. It is best to call ministers of religion such, even if from our own theological position we may believe they are preaching a false security to a people who do not have such security.

The ambassadors to Zedekiah (Jeremiah 27). This chapter tells the story of foreign ambassadors who have come to visit King Zedekiah. The MT text here differs significantly from the LXX. The Hebrew editors have expanded on the text to make a statement about Nebuchadnezzar as "my servant" (compare Jer. 25) and clarify that Nebuchadnezzar's role in God's plans is temporary. He will be punished when his time comes! The freedom with which the editors have thus added to the chapter shows again that the editors were less interested in preserving the exact words of the historical Jeremiah than in using the figure of the prophet to speak to their time. We should learn to do the same with our traditions, as the Supreme Court has done with the U.S. Constitution.

In Jerusalem, the Judean king Zedekiah is presiding over a meeting of representatives from various states in the region. (MT Jer. 27:1 places this gathering at the beginning of Jehoiakim's reign, but that may result from 26:1 having been copied to the wrong place. The LXX omits this verse, and modern English translations usually correct the name to Zedekiah, since that king is named several times in Jer. 27.) The high-level meeting in Jerusalem is evidently to plan a common strategy among the nations of the Syro-Palestinian region against the imperial control of Babylon. Ambassadors of the kings of Edom, Moab, Ammon, Tyre, and Sidon are present in Jerusalem. And they have all come with the support of their respective religious leaders, their prophets, at least according to Jeremiah.

Jeremiah makes a cross-cultural attack on the ministers of religion, representing various gods and various theologies, as false ministers. The Holy One, the God of Israel, has revealed to Jeremiah that all these nations must submit to the yoke of Nebuchadnezzar, "my servant." Those who refuse will be condemned by the Holy One to suffer the sword, famine, and pestilence (27:8). The envoys are to report to their respective kings that the ministers of religion (prophets) who say that God (whichever god) can free them from the king of Babylon are preaching a lie (27:9–10). The Holy One, who made all people and beasts, has given them all over to Babylon, which becomes therefore for the time being the divinely authorized empire. This is a truly remarkable historico-theological assessment of the geopolitical situation of that time. It can only be understood when we realize the royal theology that Jeremiah meant to undercut. This theology claimed that God had an eternal commitment to David and to the Jerusalem temple, God's resting place, and that its security was assured, regardless of greater geopolitical developments. Jeremiah's ministry was devoted to destroying that false security, a security based on a theology that was not faithful to the Torah or, we might add, to Jeroboam's revolt against David's house in the tenth century. (Jeremiah came from Anathoth, near the border between Judah and the former kingdom of Israel, and he was probably aware of the different theology that prevailed in that kingdom.)

Religion in any epoch tends to lull believers into security. Ministers of religion have a vested interest in supporting the prevailing powers. Around the world, ministers of the various religious traditions tend to support the world controlled by the great multinationals through the Market. The fact that many religious leaders nevertheless supported the global Jubilee 2000 campaign for the cancellation of international debts reveals the crisis of the Global Market, which is not supporting the life needs of a majority of today's people. The division of the Christian churches of the world before the large corporations represented by the IMF and the widely generalized opposition of Muslim religious leaders to the Global Market and its representatives reveals the crisis we face. Jeremiah was, or thought he was, a solitary voice. Today, those who oppose the IMF, the WTO, and similar representatives of big capital are no longer lonely voices in the wilderness. But they remain a minority in the total scene of religious leaders and still find it hard to have their voices taken seriously in the face of the chorus proclaiming "there is no alternative (TINA)."[1] The postexilic community rescued Jeremiah as the voice of God, after the fact. Could we begin some serious discussion of alternative economies now while the Global Market still reigns supreme? It would be a major achievement just to take the discussion seriously in those countries that benefit from the present arrangement at the price of the increasing difficulty that the vast majority have in simply surviving. Can our ministers of religion promote a destruction of the TINA consensus and a serious discussion of alternatives?

Hananiah challenges Jeremiah (Jeremiah 28). The close linkage between this chapter and the previous one is indicated from the start with the introduction, "And in that same year." Jeremiah has questioned the consensus of religious leaders at a crucial moment for the Judahite state, the international high-level conference hosted by King Zedekiah in Jerusalem. The conferees have left, presumably, with the impression that there is significant lack of control by the king over his people and its religious leaders. But by now, about thirty years into Jeremiah's prophetic ministry, Jeremiah is a senior figure as a representative prophet of the Holy One and cannot be lightly dismissed or imprisoned.

After the dust has settled, a prophet arises who challenges Jeremiah's word and instead voices the majority opinion among Jerusalem's religious leaders. Hananiah's name means "God is merciful." We should probably not assume that he was an opportunist who voiced the king's opinion because this was the way to get ahead in Jerusalem. He may well have been convinced that the Holy One of Israel was indeed a merciful God wishing only good for Judah. Precedent supported him. One hundred years before, in 701 B.C.E., Jerusalem had been besieged by a most powerful Assyrian army in the days of Hezekiah and had been miraculously delivered when God sent a plague among the Assyrian troops. The prophet Isaiah had preached that Zion would be the gathering place of the nations, and the law would be taught to them so that all could live in peace (Isa. 2:1–5). Isaiah had encouraged Hezekiah during the dark days of the Assyrian attack and had been vindicated by the outcome of that conflict. With all of this and the great promises to David delivered by Nathan five centuries before, Hananiah was emboldened to challenge the veteran prophet Jeremiah. Hananiah's message was simple: The Holy One would soon free Jerusalem from the Babylonian menace and bring back the temple implements that Nebuchadnezzar had taken away. The Holy One would bring back the young king Jeconiah and those who were exiled with him (Jer. 28:4). As a dramatic symbol of his message, Hananiah broke the yoke that Jeremiah used to demonstrate subjugation to Babylon.

Jeremiah's response to this challenge from a presumably younger colleague is complex and merits analysis. The "Amen" (Jer. 28:6) should probably be understood as heavy with sarcasm. Hananiah was voicing a majority opinion that Jeremiah had challenged in the imposing setting of the international congress. It is not likely that this prophecy convinced Jeremiah to change his mind, though no doubt he, like all Judahites, shared a secret hope that God would somehow intervene on their behalf. There may thus have been an element of hope in the expression, "May the Holy One do so" (28:6). Should God lift the Babylonian stranglehold on Judah and the neighboring nations and should Nebuchadnezzar return the implements he took from the temple, everything Jeremiah had been saying for the last ten years would be proven wrong. It would require nothing less than a conversion on Jeremiah's part to genuinely accept the short-term hope that Hananiah and the rest of the religious establishment were holding out to the people of Jerusalem. The sobering words that follow the wish expressed in 28:6 demonstrate that Jeremiah has suffered nothing like a conversion. He still represents a Torah theology, which does not deny the Holy One's mercy but places that mercy in a complex divine personality that also demands and judges, requiring that kings do acts of justice and that judges liberate the oppressed, and backing this requirement with harsh judgments. Precedents, declares Jeremiah in 28:7–8, are not in favor of Hananiah and his royal theology. The prophets have (always?) announced pestilence, war, and famine against nations and kingdoms. He is thinking, no doubt, of Hosea, Amos, Micah, Habakkuk, and lesser figures. When you preach peace in troubled times, your message must be tested by the trial of time. When what you say comes about we can believe you. Until then, we must reserve our judgment.

All this is simplified on both sides of the issue, of course. Neither Jeremiah's remarks nor Hananiah's can be taken as the only truth about history. History resists generalizations, and one cannot automatically assume that the outcome of a Babylonian invasion under Nebuchadnezzar will echo the outcome of the Assyrian invasion under Sennacherib. Nor can one be confident that liberation struggles in Colombia or Chechneya will be as successful as the Cuban and Vietnamese national liberation struggles. The lessons of history are complex, and the actions of God mysterious.

Jeremiah holds his ground even though he avoids a direct public confrontation with his challenger. Eventually, he appears in public with a new yoke, this one made of iron rather than wood. (The "sometime after" of Jer. 28:12 in NRSV, suggesting a lapse of time, is deceptive; neither the Hebrew nor the Greek suggest any lapse of time.) While it would be impractical to do real work with a yoke of iron, the strong metal makes a point for Jeremiah. God's will that Judah submit to Babylon is firm and will not be altered.

By the time this prose narrative was compiled, after the Babylonian exile, it was evident that Hananiah and most of Zedekiah's religious advisors had been whistling in the dark. God had not intervened to save Judah and Jerusalem from imperial control. The sins of kings, priests, and prophets fell on their children with all the weight of a righteous God who would not ignore wrongdoing or let the evildoer off the hook. Jeremiah's lonely prophetic stance was vindicated by history. But we, now, cannot wait for the verdict of history. We must act in the present, when the facts are still not clear. Is TINA correct, and are the protestors at Seattle and Genoa beating against a wall? Who are the true prophets of God today? Are they the pastors who preach that all is well in today's world, and that all we have to do is send more shipments of food to the starving people of Chad and Haiti, or are they the dissidents who call for cancellation of debts by New York and Berlin banks and for radical revamping of the Market, especially the financial markets? We cannot wait for time to tell. We must discern the will of God today. Our lives are short, and the verdict of history may not come until we are safely buried six feet under the surface. As ministers of religion, we must speak the word of God today. We cannot assume that God's will always supports the status quo, but neither can we assume that God always opposes it. (God cannot be a permanent nonconformist or we would never have a satisfactory social system.) We must discern the circumstances of our time. This is a task for every believer, and more so for every minister of religion.

Jeremiah Addresses the Babylonian Exile Community (Jeremiah 29)

This chapter addresses the exiles who were taken with Jeconiah (also known as Jehoiachin) to Babylon in 597 B.C.E. In both the structural balance of the book and in theme, it corresponds to the vision of the two baskets of figs in Jeremiah 24. The book of Jeremiah places the future of God's people with this first exilic community, not with those exiled in 586 B.C.E. with King Zedekiah. The Jeremiah tradition was edited by people who returned to Jerusalem from Babylon after Cyrus of Persia captured Babylon in 539 B.C.E. They apparently felt themselves to be descendants of the first exile that was, according to Jeremiah 52:28–32, the largest of the three deportations from Jerusalem to Babylon. Chapters 24 and 29 provide some of the clearest evidence of this origin for the Jeremiah tradition. They give us a Jeremiah who is pro-Babylonian and who sees the first exile as the genuine continuation of the people of God, whom God is punishing with exile but whom God will restore at the right moment in God's governance of the world.

We have observed a fundamental ideological divide between Jeremiah and the political and religious establishment of Jerusalem, represented by the priests and especially by the prophets. In this chapter, we find a similar divide between Jeremiah and the prophets of the exilic community in Babylon. The adherents to Davidic promise theology are now divided into a group supporting the exiled king Jehoiachin and a group supporting Zedekiah in Jerusalem. Prophets in both groups believe that the Holy One will save the city from destruction right quick. But Jeremiah, who believes in a stern God who will not let sins and rebellions go unpunished, announces to both the exiles and those who remain in Jerusalem that the city's fall to Babylon is inevitable. Jeremiah 29 presents itself as a sort of pastoral letter from Jeremiah to the exilic community in Babylon. The letter is carried by Elasah, a son of the scribe Shaphan, who was behind King Josiah's reform (see 2 Kings 22—23). The expedition with which Elasah traveled was financed by King Zedekiah and presumably carried far more than the prophet's letter.

Jeremiah's advice is remarkable. The exiles are to settle down and make a life for themselves in the foreign place. They are to build houses, plant vineyards, marry their daughters off, and receive wives for their sons. This must have been painful advice for people who were mostly government bureaucrats, not farmers. They are not to listen to prophets who promise that God will restore them to Jerusalem—such promises are lies, not messages from God. Jeremiah says that the exile will be seventy years long, a way of saying that neither they nor their children will know anything else. The exiles must adjust to a modest life in a foreign land, after being an urban elite in Jerusalem, but God will be with them. The Holy One wishes you well and not harm (29:11), Jeremiah tells them, but your welfare is for your lifetimes tied up with Babylon.

Furthermore, you have a mission in your new home. You must pray to the Holy One for the welfare of Babylon. In its welfare will be your welfare (29:7). Life is short and historical time is not measured by human lifetimes. We may have no doubt that the Global Market will collapse because of its inability to feed and provide for the basic needs of people. But we must recognize that we are not talking about our lifetimes. For the time being, the Market is remarkably healthy, in spite of occasional crises like the Mexican financial crisis of the early 1990s, the later problem with the stock markets of Southeast Asia, and the recent Argentine political and economic crisis. The Market is quite resilient and capable of dealing with its own crises, in spite of its inability to provide for people's needs. In today's situation, God's people must learn to live with this Market, and even to pray for it and its leaders. Its welfare is also the welfare of the people of God, even when it condemns some of them to inhuman poverty. In the short run, the advocates of TINA are right. The alternatives are for the future, as Jeremiah assured the Babylonian exiles. In such a situation, the exiles must keep the hope alive. The scribal training that is useless in rural Babylon will be needed when the day of God's promise comes true. We, also, must plan for the hopeful future when an alternative to the Global Market becomes a real possibility and teach our congregations and our children to keep the fires of hope burning, even while they pray for the short-term success of the Market.

As in chapters 25 and 27, we find evidence for editorial modification at the last stage of the text's development. The whole condemnation of the remnant not taken into exile (Jer. 29:16–20) was added in the last revision (it is not present in LXX). It obviously reflects the returned exiles' desire to exclude persons who, they felt, were unworthy to share in the construction of the new nation under Persian auspices. We have previously noted the valuable additions of the latest of the editors of Jeremiah, but this addition reflects an unfortunate use of religion against the "other." Today's Christians similarly use biblical statements about exclusive salvation in the name of

Jesus (Acts 4:12; Rom. 10:9–13) to disqualify Muslims, Jews, or Hindus from full acceptance in international affairs.

The latter part of the chapter deals with specific prophetic opponents of Jeremiah: Ahab and Zedekiah in Jeremiah 29:21–23, and Shemaiah in 29:24–32. In Shemaiah's case, the prophetic rivalry draws in advocates of both Jehoiachin and Zedekiah. The Judean and Babylonian Jewish communities can still join hands when it becomes a matter of silencing a common enemy. But when the priest Zephaniah receives the letter calling for detention and public dishonoring of Jeremiah, he only reads it to him privately and does not follow its instructions. Apparently, Jeremiah himself had followed his own advice and made friends among the "enemy," although for Jeremiah the "enemy" is the Jerusalem religious establishment. Jeremiah counseled the exiles to pray for the welfare of the people among whom they lived, and we know from earlier chapters (12—15) that, in spite of the Holy One's prohibition, Jeremiah himself continued to pray for the welfare of the people among whom he lived, the people of Jerusalem, though he believed the city would soon fall by the "sword, hunger, and pestilence."

We believers know that God is loving and merciful. Christians say with John that "God is love" (1 Jn. 4:8). Muslims begin every prayer with the confession called 'al fatiha, "In the name of God, the Clement, the Merciful." This does not mean that God is not stern with sinners or that God does not call nations to account for their evil deeds. Jeremiah was convinced that Jerusalem would be destroyed, but he was equally convinced that God's plans for the people were well-being and not harm (Jer. 29:11). This is the God in whom we believe, and what Jeremiah counsels the exiles in Babylon is also the way of true religion in the twenty-first century.

PART E'

A New Covenant and New Prophetic Role
(Jeremiah 30—33)

These four chapters of Jeremiah form a distinctive block. Most of the book of Jeremiah is made up of oracles of judgment or narratives that relate incidents having to do with the judgments of the Holy One of Israel on Jerusalem, Judah, and the nations, especially Babylon. This corresponds to the announcement made in Jeremiah 1:10 that Jeremiah is sent to pluck up and pull down, to destroy and to overthrow. But that text also says that Jeremiah is to build and to plant. These positive themes show up elsewhere in the book of Jeremiah in only a few minor statements, but they dominate Jeremiah 30—33. So, these four chapters stand out as the prophet's positive vision for the future, when God will call God's people back from the ends of the earth where God has scattered them. It is impossible to determine how much of this comes from the prophet himself. Most of it probably comes from later followers of the Jeremiah tradition, but there is no reason to think that Jeremiah himself thought Babylon and exile would be the absolute end of Judah and of Israel. So, there may well be something in these chapters that goes back to Jeremiah, but determining which parts might have originated with the prophet himself is a hopeless task. In its present canonical form, the book is of one piece, and we will interpret it as such.

Within the whole of the book with its ring structure, this section corresponds to chapters 11—20. Jeremiah 31:31–34 on the new covenant corresponds to Jeremiah 11:1–13 on the original covenant, which was established when God redeemed Israel from bondage in Egypt and led it to Sinai to reveal there the Torah. The rest of Jeremiah 11:14—20:18 is a series of oracles of judgment against Judah, sprinkled with some personal prayers of lamentation protesting the prophet's fate of exclusion from ordinary social life in Judah. Our present section also contains a personal element, when God orders the prophet to buy a property in Anathoth as a sign and signal of God's will to again have normal transactions in the land (32:1–15). For the rest, the negative statements about the judgments of God in chapters 11—20 are counterweighted by the positive announcements of hope in chapters 30—33.

Chapters 30—33 are divided between poetry (Jer. 30—31) and prose (Jer. 32—33). Both sections have to do with hope and restoration, so it seems proper to treat them as one section, which is surely what the editors of the book intended readers to do. As we would expect for sayings on the gathering in and return from exile that have been reworked in the tradition, we find considerable divergence between MT and LXX, especially in the prose sections. This confirms the natural suspicion that these chapters were more heavily reworked by the editors than were the sayings of judgment against Judah and against the nations. Though this commentary does not systematically enter into textual matters, which are best reserved for readers of the Hebrew and Greek texts, I will have occasion to comment on some of these "last minute" adaptations of the tradition revealed in the differences between LXX and MT. (I have posited that the LXX represents an older form of the tradition than does MT, see earlier pp. 4–5.) Surely, for readers of the book at the time of the reconstruction of Jerusalem and Judah in the days of Nehemiah and Ezra, these sections must have seemed especially important and relevant.

They may seem less important and relevant to us today. I have proposed that if we are to take the book of Jeremiah as Holy Scripture, the Word of God, we must read it not just as a book about Judah and Babylon in the sixth century B.C.E., but as a book about empires in general. Today, the book speaks to Jewish people and Christian churches in their complex relation with today's empire, the United States. The relation is especially complex because most churches have a significant portion of their membership in the United States, where they are pressured by patriotism to support military adventures, which are the most direct expression of imperialism today and always. Jewish people are, for the most part, committed to support the State of Israel, which serves as a beachhead of empire in the oil-rich Middle East. Today's Israel survives on the basis of a very large military budget supplied by the United States. So, today's people or peoples of God are intimately tied to empire as were only a small minority of the scribes employed by the Babylonian state in Jeremiah's time. The chapters we are now exploring deal with a time when that empire will no longer exist or will be diminished to the level of any ordinary state, and the scattered people of God will be again gathered in the promised land with a rebuilt Jerusalem. This also has a correspondence today.

One of the most striking things about the global situation today is the dramatic distance between the rich and the poor. These differences do not correspond to the differences between the nations of the United States, Europe, and Japan, on the one hand, and the rest of the world on the other. In every country of the world, there exist very wealthy people who invest their money in New York banks, or those in Tokyo or Zurich, and who travel regularly to do their shopping and vacationing in Miami or Paris or Hong Kong. However, the poor are a much larger and more visible sector in the Southern countries, so we can speak in a general way about the divide between the North and the South, although we should not take this too literally. It is said that today the wealthiest 20 percent of the world's population controls sixty times the resources of the poorest 20 percent. This percentage has increased dramatically in the last forty years, from a time when the proportion was closer to two to one. This immensely unjust distribution, especially in the light of the fact that much of that poorest 20 percent does not have the resources to assure food or medicines to their children, is only possible in the last instance because of the military might of the empire. There are other contributing causes, such as the grossly undemocratic fashion in which business enterprises are run within countries that pride themselves on their political democracies, but, without military means, the inequalities could not be sustained. In this context, our return from dispersion must be understood as the elimination of unnecessary military expenses in the United States and the democratization of business enterprises everywhere, so that this world can become a place designed for human living in just societies. Until that happens, or at least until a process is under way to reach that goal, the people of God must feel dispersed and exiled in an alien world. We are still in "exile."

With this background we are now ready to turn to Jeremiah 30—33, texts that are quite different from what we have read up until now in the book of Jeremiah.

Turning the Captivity (Jeremiah 30:1–11)

This segment includes at least two subsections. Jeremiah 30:1–3 introduces chapters 30—33, placing the whole under the caption of "turning the captivity" (*shuv et-shevuth* or *shuv shevuth*). The problem addressed here is the Babylonian captivity of the people of "Israel and Judah." Some have interpreted this as pointing to the deportation of Samaria and Israel by the Assyrians in 721 B.C.E. While some of Jeremiah's own poems may have addressed that situation, both the caption (Israel *and Judah*) and the content of Jeremiah 30—31 make plain that the present text refers to the later Babylonian captivity and the general dispersion that was a fact by the sixth century B.C.E.

It could be argued that Jeremiah 30:4–11 should be subdivided. The general theme is the terror of destruction and dispersion (30:4–7) and the promise of return to the land and peace there (30:8–11). The opening image is dramatic: There is no peace, and there is something new on the face of the earth, men who hold their bellies in pain just like women in labor, except that it is a useless pain, for there is no childbirth as reward. A quick statement at the end of the poem assures the listener that Jacob will be rescued from this distress. LXX Jeremiah does not include verses 10–11, which means that the piece ends with the substitution of "service" to God in the place of service to the enemies of Judah (verse 9). The verses added in MT have the effect of relating the promised new situation specifically to the gathering of the dispersed people from the various lands to which God had dispersed them. It is a powerful statement that much strengthens the whole. Without these verses, the oracle is dominated by the figure of males writhing in pains like those of childbirth (30:6), but, with it, emphasis shifts to the promise of the broken yoke (30:8–9).

This oracle as a whole (verses 4–11) is an assurance that the powerful empire's grip will be broken, and Judah's scattered people will be restored. How can the prophet predict this unlikely outcome of history? Obviously, this is not a political or sociological analysis. It all depends on the fidelity of God, the God who promises, "I will make an end to the nations among which I dispersed you" (30:11). In other words, God is in charge, both in the dispersal and in the subsequent gathering. The nations, especially Babylon, will come to their end. This is nothing more than God's declaration. In today's secularized world, listeners expect some political analysis to back up such unlikely statements. Who says that empire will come to an end? And on the basis of what debilitating factors that are present in today's reality? Obviously, it is possible to make a general statement that the U.S. empire will one day end, just on the basis of the finitude of all things earthly.

It is an absolutely certain statement even if no date is given to the end. All human institutions die sooner or later, and there is no reason to believe that the U.S. empire is an exception. But the prophet's statement amounts to more than this. A proximate timetable has been announced in Jeremiah 29, "seventy years." Instead of a political analysis, this oracle offers a moral one: "I will punish in just measure, though I will not leave iniquity unpunished" (Jer. 30:11). If one believes, as Jeremiah does, that God rules the movements of history, the logical next step is to announce, as the prophetic text does here, that this governance is not arbitrary and that events punish and reward nations in just measure. So, there is a moral sentence pending over the apparently mighty Babylonian empire. Whether or not one believes in the morality of historical developments is a difficult problem in the context of contemporary rationality. We can at least understand the "ought" character of such judgments, whether they apply to political developments or not. We can believe that U.S. empire that supports the free movement of financial capital and strictly controls the movements of humans, especially poor humans, ought to be destroyed, though we may have no political reasons to give us assurance that it will be in the short run. The prophet is satisfied to be assured that God has promised that Babylon will be destroyed and Israel restored to its land, free to worship God according to the Torah. Maybe this is the best we can do today.

An Incurable Disease Cured (Jeremiah 30:12–17)

This is a simple poem with a powerful message. God says, to an individual feminine addressee (probably Jerusalem), You have a wound that is incurable. There is no medicine capable of treating it and no healing possible. "Your" lovers (or friends) have abandoned you in your deplorable state. "I" struck you with the blow of an enemy because of your numerous sins. Why do you cry out? I did it because of the multitude of your sins (this verse, 15, is not in the LXX). The "therefore" (which NIV softens to the expected "but") in Jeremiah 30:16 is somewhat surprising. In prophetic speech, this word usually introduces the sentence of judgment after the listing of sins. Here, sins and a wound have been mentioned, and it is time for the sentence to be passed against the accused. But no! What we now have is a sentence against the abusers of Israel, in a whole series of inversions (v. 16). "I" will restore health to "you" (again feminine singular), the one whose wound was just declared incurable. As in the previous oracle (30:4–11), we have the emergence of historical novelty as a result of God's unexpected action. This is grace, God's merciful action for no reason one can cite except God's mercy and God's ability to do a new thing.

Jerusalem Shall be Restored as a Place of Mirth
(Jeremiah 30:18–24)

This section poetically describes the mirth that will be again known in Jerusalem when God restores "her" to her former glory. This is described as a restoration (*shuv shevuth*, the general expression characteristic of Jeremiah 30—31), but it is also a return, using the same verb (*shuv*) that the prophets use for repentance (as a turning from evil to the straight paths of justice).

Central to the restoration of Israel's fortunes is the rebuilding of the city Jerusalem. In this poem, we also have the restoration of kingship, that is, political institutions that enable life to be carried out in a normal fashion. (Actually, the poet/prophet avoids the term king and uses a more general word for leader, *'addir*, conventionally and somewhat misleadingly translated "prince"). Then, we have the theme statement of covenant, "you shall be my people and I shall be your God," a statement we first encountered in the covenant passage in Jeremiah 11. This is a fitting conclusion for a poem about restoring the people and their institutions to the happy state they knew before their dispersal among the nations.

The last two verses of this chapter form a reflective addition that is not really part of the preceding poem. A general statement is made here about the effectiveness of the word of God, which will definitely accomplish the purposes for which it was issued. It will become a storm against the enemies of God and of Jerusalem.

Israel Will Be Gathered from the Nations (Jeremiah 31:1–14)

Jeremiah 31:1–14 consists of an introduction (31:1) and two poems (31:2–6 and 31:7–14), all having the same general theme. Like other poems gathered in chapter 31, these are oracles of salvation, promising hope to a people scattered in many places and despairing of maintaining their identity. The poems are introduced with a general statement that picks up the covenant formula we have found several times in Jeremiah: I will be their [or your] God and they [or you] shall be my people.

The poem that begins the collection centers around the everlasting love of God for Israel (Jer. 31:3). There is no further motive for God's gracious actions for Israel beyond this love. This "love forever," this *hesed* (steadfast love, loving kindness, mercy, faithfulness), is inexplicable, a divine mystery. God's love for Israel (or the Christian church) cannot be explained by a supposed virtue superior to that of other peoples, for there is no special virtue to this people. To state the paradox, some theologians (Leonardo Boff and others) speak of the church as a "chaste whore." The expression, though not original to Leonardo Boff, was made current in today's theology by *Boff's Iglesia, carisma y poder* (1982), the book that provoked the Vatican to impose a year of silence on Boff in 1985-1986. This could certainly apply just as well to the people Israel or to the Jewish people today. Religion often seems like a prized product that is sold to the best offer on the political market. And yet, there is something holy and separate about this people and this religious institution. In the end, we can do no better than to declare the mysterious eternal love and equally mysterious fidelity of God to them.

The planting of fruit on the hills of Samaria (31:5) assures the material quality of the salvation promised. This is not a promise for a heavenly compensation but for a restoration in the land from which God expelled Israel.

After Lamentation, Newness of Life (Jeremiah 31:15–30)

Here I group together three sayings (31:15–22, 23–26, and 27–30) that continue the general theme of restoration we have met in the previous two sayings.

The first poem begins with the disconsolate weeping of Rachel for her children that are no more. In his desperation, Ephraim, one of Rachel's "children," recognizes that he has been a stubborn calf and pleads for restoration to God's mercies. God is moved by love for a "precious son" (31:20), in language that recalls God's maternal womb. (The verb *rhm,* "to love, to have compassion for," used in the last line of this verse, is derived from the Hebrew noun for womb.) Today, such images supply a powerful tool for renovating our language about God, which has become worn with too much reliance on father language. This poem ends with a call to fix road markers to show the way back. The people are named a "rebellious daughter" (31:22). It all ends with the enigmatic statement in verse 22b, "a female encompasses a male." The meaning of this is not at all clear; perhaps it was not intended to make a clear statement. One can at least say that the ending of the poem in Jeremiah 31:15–22 promises a new social order where the relations of female and male will not be traditional. Israel's restoration will not be a simple reinstatement of the old status quo, but the inauguration of something new.

The next saying (31:23–26) appears to be prose, literary prose tinged with poetic solemnity. Judging by the final statement about awaking and finding the sleep pleasant, the vision of herders and tillers of the soil carrying out their tasks peacefully in Judah is the prophet's dream. Likewise, the Holy One's blessing with a legitimate home (literally, "rightful pasture") and holy hill (verse 23) are to be understood as part of the prophet's dream.

Dreaming is an important activity, whether in sleep or what we call daydreaming, when daily reality is let out of consciousness to make room for dreams of a better world that might be. Unless our prophets and our poets dream of a new and better world, we will surely be stuck in the present one, with all its serious defects.

The third saying (31:27–30) is also a prose statement, built up as a reflection on the prophet's call in Jeremiah 1:10. Until now, the prophet has undertaken to pluck up, tear down, overthrow, destroy, and bring evil. Now, God certifies that his call is also to build and to plant, items neglected until this point. An end to the saying about the parents eating sour grapes and causing dental problems for the children is a freeing message for the generation that Cyrus allows to return to Judah (Ezra 1). It comes, evidently, from the latter stages of the writing of this prophetic book. All the prophetic books in the Bible show marks of editorial work that picks up prophetic sayings issued in the context of a declining monarchy and spices them with sayings like this one, encouraging the generation that feels the ancestors' guilt as an intolerable burden. The Jeremiah tradition assures its later readers that they need no longer worry about old sins, which have been purged with exile and dispersion.

God Offers New Covenant to House of Israel and House of Judah (Jeremiah 31:31–34)

Within the book of Jeremiah, this offer of a new covenant serves to balance Jeremiah 11:1–14, which speaks of the covenant with the fathers when the Holy One brought them out of Egypt, out of the house of bondage. As Jeremiah has tirelessly repeated since chapter 11, the people of Israel and the people of Judah have forfeited that covenant by their repeated sinning against the Torah given by God at Sinai. Now, among the list of marvelous new deeds that God will do to restore the scattered people, is the offer of a new covenant to replace and perfect the one offered to the ancestors.

The newness of this new covenant is defined in several ways. (1) There will be a genuine relation between God and Israel, as God becomes in fact a God for the people and they a people for God (Jer. 31:33). (2) There will be genuine "knowledge of God," which must mean both knowledge of the salvation history and the sort of knowledge that Josiah showed when he acted justly and made good judicial decisions (Jer. 22:15–16). (3) Access to this "knowledge" will be shared by all in a "democratic" fashion without elitism. No one will teach neighbor, brother, or sister. Instead, *God will write* the Torah directly on the hearts (Jer. 31:33–34). The newness is not *that* the Torah is to be written on the heart, but *who* will do the writing. Because God will write it, the people will no longer be dependent on the priests, prophets, and other elite leaders. (4) All this will be so because God will forgive their sins and remember them no more (Jer. 31:34). Marvelous and glorious novelty!

But new as this covenant may be, we must not forget that in the context of Jeremiah 30—31, these "new" deeds of God are for the benefit of the people whom God will call to return from the many countries where God has scattered them. It is with the reconstituted people of Israel and Judah that God will do the deed of healing the incurable wound and replacing the broken covenant with a new and better one.

This last point is an important one for readers of this commentary, most of whom will surely be Christian. Once, at Sinai, the Holy One suggested to Moses that he step aside so that God could destroy the people of Israel and give him, Moses, a new people who would not have stiff necks (Ex. 32:7–14). When Moses rejected that suggestion as unacceptable, God seems never again to have suggested such a preposterous thing. God is committed to this Jewish people, regardless of how irrational and particularistic this may appear to others. Paul in his letter to the Romans (11:1–6) makes this point by citing the permanence of the election of the Jews as a sign of God's fidelity to God's own promises. If the permanence of the covenant with Israel depended on the fulfilment of the Torah, then the grace of God who is merciful without needing a corresponding fidelity would be cancelled. By no means! says Paul. Should God change partners for this new covenant, as some Christian preachers suggest, the fidelity of God would be abandoned and with it the hope that rests on God's promises.

So, what do we say about the sustained argument of the letter to the Hebrews in the New Testament (Heb. 8:8–13)? Here, an anonymous author declares the first covenant obsolete and disappearing (Heb. 8:13). This author believes that the Christian movement, later church, will displace and replace the Jewish people. The least we can say is that after twenty centuries during which the Jewish people have survived multiple persecutions, even catastrophic ones, this view has been disproved. The Jewish people, with their dogged persistence in the "first" covenant, to use Hebrews' expression, have proven that God has sustained them through thick and thin. And as we have seen, in the book of Jeremiah the promises of these chapters are addressed not to Gentiles, but to the people God intends to call back from the exile and dispersion. If anything, the vision in Hebrews turns out to be the "old" one that must be displaced. Of course, this must not mean that Jeremiah's text applies only to the Jewish people and not to the Christian church as well. We Christians also need an ever-renewed covenant with our God in which our sins are again forgiven. In a Christian church that threatens to become frozen in hierarchical structures that reduce lay persons to purely passive roles, we Christians also need to recover the egalitarianism of God's promise. We all need renewal of our knowledge of God, both our catechistic knowledge and our knowledge through actions of justice and right. May God be with us to make this ever so!

Indissolubility of God's Commitment to God's People (Jeremiah 31:35–40)

This final text of chapter 31 is really two pieces, a poem in verses 35–37 and a prose promise for the latter days in verses 38–40.

The poem compares the fidelity of God's commitment to Israel with the fixed order of the sun, moon, and stars in the sky. "If the heavens can be measured or the foundations of the earth explored, then I will reject the children of Israel for the deeds they have done" (31:37). There are, in God's world, certain fixed decrees—what we might call "natural laws"—and the commitment to Israel is just as firm as these.

The prose passage (verses 38–40) is a straightforward promise for Jerusalem for the "latter days." The places mentioned are unknown to us but show that the editors of this book were intimately familiar with the city and its surroundings. Thus, the promises of new things in chapters 30 and 31 are anchored in the earthy specificity of the city that the Jewish people have loved and continue to love. This is, of course, problematic today, when for fourteen centuries Muslims have also venerated the holy mount from which Muhammad ascended to heaven in a vision. Insofar as we seek a world governed by the knowledge of God that is the practice of justice, solutions to Jerusalem must be sought that respect the historic claims of both Muslims and Jews to these holy sites. We must contribute to the U.N. efforts to withdraw this city from the sphere of military conflict, where matters are solved by military might regardless of claims of justice, and seek a more lasting peace based on justice.

Concrete Hope: Buy a Field! (Jeremiah 32:1–44)

Here, we encounter a long chapter in prose. It deals with judgment, the dominant theme of the book, but also with the hope of restoration, the theme of chapters 30—33. The most remarkable thing about this chapter of hope is its basis in a concrete transaction, the purchase of a piece of land by a convict in a city surrounded by imperial armies. This improbable transaction becomes a perfect symbol of God's determination to be gracious to God's people! The whole chapter focuses on this transaction, which is described in full legal detail in Jeremiah 32:6–15. Verses 1–5 set the scene, placing the prophet in jail and the Babylonian army around the city in the tenth year of King Zedekiah, the eighteenth of Nebuchadnezzar, king of Babylon. In Jeremiah 32:16–25, Jeremiah's prayer underscores the improbability, even impossibility, of God's order and God's promise. Verses 26–44 give God's own theological reflection on this momentous occasion in Israel's history and its impossibilities, which are possibilities for God.

First, the setting. The chapter opens, like many other chapters of the book of Jeremiah, promising a word from God. The chapter does indeed have a word from God, eventually, but the first word it offers is from the king, who has just confined Jeremiah in prison. This word, Jeremiah 32:3b-5, shows that King Zedekiah has indeed listened to Jeremiah, so much so that he can quote accurately the substance of his preaching: I, God, am going to give the city into the hands of the Babylonian army; the king will not escape but will be taken to Babylon to stay. Zedekiah is upset by the message. Despite the old saying, "Sticks and stones may break my bones, but words can do me no harm," governments know that words are in fact powerful instruments, which is why governments everywhere seek to control words, one way or another. Newspapers are closed down when they are continuously critical and governments find no way to control them. During a war, armies do their best to control the press and limit it to official releases. One of the "successes" of the 1991 Gulf War against Iraq, from the U.S. Army's point of view, was that the press was excluded from the battlefield, getting all its information from the Army's own press officers. The 2003 invasion was handled differently, with "imbedded reporters" but to the same effect, to have news reports that reflected the army's point of view. Before the days of newspapers and television news, prophets were a way of gaining independent information and views on happenings of the day. And so it was that Zedekiah had Jeremiah confined to jail, where he was not able to deliver his message to the people. Zedekiah knew perfectly well what Jeremiah was saying, as his quotation shows, and so the imprisonment was no accident but a premeditated political action. This is the setting for this chapter.

Imprisoned or free, Jeremiah maintained his contact with the source of his message, the Holy One of Israel. In prison, God gave him a surprisingly specific order to buy a field in Anathoth (Jeremiah's hometown) that his father's brother was putting up for sale. In a war situation, properties become worthless, or nearly so, because the future is so unpredictable. It is a buyer's market, if the seller can even find a fool so blissfully ignorant as to wish to buy land. But the Holy One orders Jeremiah, who has no idea what will become of him as a prisoner in a war-torn city, to purchase the land! He is to follow all the customary legal proceedings of a property transaction to keep land in the extended family, with moneys weighed and documents signed in the presence of witnesses, as if these were normal times. The transaction thus becomes a statement by God's imprisoned prophet that a normal economy lies in Judah's future. Property will again be sold and bought in Judah. This text introduces a scribe, a sort of notary, who will in coming chapters assume a greater role in Jeremiah's prophetic ministry. This is Baruch ("blessed one"), son of Neriah, whose brother Seraiah will play a similar role with another document of hope at the end of the book (Jer. 51:59–64).

Jeremiah's prayer in Jeremiah 32:16–25 is remarkable. The Holy One's creative deeds are attributed to God's "great power and outstretched arm," an expression usually used in the context of the exodus (Ex. 6:6; 15:16; Deut. 4:34, 5:15; 7:19; and elsewhere). Jeremiah's phrasing thus brings to mind God's deeds before Pharoah to bring the children of Israel out of Egypt. This initial confession climaxes in the affirmation that "nothing is too marvelous for you" (32:17). This in turn calls to mind the affirmations made to Sarah when she laughed at the idea that she might bear a child in her old age. God responds in Gen. 18:14, "Is anything too wonderful for the Holy One?" (The LXX translates this phrase in Jeremiah as "nothing is hidden," though the MT is surely a stronger statement, "nothing is too wonderful.") The reference to the wonders of the exodus becomes explicit in Jeremiah 32:20–23, which also introduces the theme of the gift of the land. Yet, Jeremiah knows, the people have brought disaster upon themselves by disobedience. He concludes in verse 25 with an incredulous question: "And yet, you say to me, Buy land…though the city is given into the hands of the Chaldeans?" So, the prayer is a confession of faith that elicits from God an explanation, while expressing no doubt about God's ability to do anything.

God's answer accepts Jeremiah's affirmation that nothing is too marvelous for God (Jer. 32:27; again LXX has "nothing is hidden"). God then recites, rather surprisingly, the human misdeeds that have provoked God to destroy Jerusalem and give it into the hands of Babylon. Such judgments are included among the wonderful deeds of which God is capable! God does indeed show steadfast mercy to thousands but also requites the sins of ancestors upon their descendants (Jer. 32:18, a reference to Ex. 20:5–6; 34:6–7). This contradictory affirmation cannot be harmonized, either in the Sinai revelation or in the living of the experience with God in Jeremiah's and Zedekiah's time. For Christians, this is the mystery of the resurrection of Jesus Christ on Sunday, which comes only after the death on the cross on Friday. For Jews, it is the revelation at Sinai; for Christians, the Friday and Sunday of Holy Week. In both cases, we must deal with a God of both judgment and mercy, whose mercy is only possible after the judgment.

And now, God continues to address the people of Judah and Jerusalem in the person of Jeremiah. The God who brought disaster on this people will now bring upon them good fortune (Jer. 32:42). The purchase of the field makes this concrete, assuring that amid the discontinuity of judgment and hope, dispersion and gathering in, there will also be continuity. God is dealing with the same people and the same land. Christians make a similar affirmation about the resurrection, which reverses Pilate's verdict and affirms Jesus whom Pilate crucified. When Thomas puts his hands into the wounds (Jn 20:24–29) there can be no doubt: it is the same body of the same person! Jeremiah's purchase of the field in Anathoth assures the people that both the judgment before their eyes and the hope expressed by the purchase of the field have to do with the same people of God in their dealing with the same Holy One, who both judges and shows forth grace. It is a wondrous confession, too wonderful for us ever to understand fully!

A Collection of Oracles that Promise Salvation (Jeremiah 33:1–26)

The Jeremiah collection of poems, narrative and prayer, and oracles that promise salvation culminates in this chapter. Interpreters, at least recent ones, regard this collection as some of the last material to be added to the book of Jeremiah. This coheres with the fact that LXX ends at verse 13, which suggests that verses 14–26 were added by MT as a sort of last-minute expansion of the promises. Notice that this addition includes promises of eternal descendants to David and to Levi, promises that are out of touch with the rest of the Jeremiah tradition (compare Jer. 22:1—23:8). In the rest of the Jeremiah tradition, the injustice of the Davidic kings leads to threats of a prompt end to that dynasty. But when the exiles were released and permission given for those who so desired to return, the hopes for the restoration of the Davidic dynasty revived, appealing to traditions of an "eternal covenant with David" (2 Sam. 7 and Ps. 89). The promise of perpetuity to Levi does not have the same anchorage in tradition. It probably reflects the political realities of life in Judah under Persian domination, when the priests were the intermediaries for Persian control in the province of Judah. When Cyrus took Babylon (539 B.C.E.), he allowed the return of the exiled Judeans (see Ezra 1) and, as the province was organized, the priests were given a privileged place in its administration.

The restoration of Jerusalem and Judah is posed on two different planes. In 33:1–13, we have the sphere of daily life, where there will be a restoration of mirth and song, which had disappeared from desolate Jerusalem after the destruction wrought by the Babylonian army. There will again be flocks of sheep and other animals tended by their shepherds in fields that had been without humans and without animals, to all effects dead and now restored to life. Verse 13 reverses the earlier threats (Jer. 7:34; 16:9; 25:10) that mirth and joy will cease in Jerusalem, which will no longer hear the voice of the bridegroom and the bride. Now the people are promised that this silence will cease and the sounds of domestic joy will again resound in the streets of Jerusalem.

The addition in MT (33:14–26) adds another promise, that the institutions for governing social life—kingship and priesthood—will be restored. Every society requires a few institutions to function adequately. Without these institutions, Judean life would be fragile and unable to survive. Assurance is here given that God would sooner break the covenant with day and night than the covenants with David and with Levi (33:20–21). The understanding here is that the succession of day and night is not, as we imagine today, "natural" and independent of God's explicit action; rather, God every day sends the sun forth and every night withdraws it so that the creatures may rest for the labors of the next day. Israel's experience with this covenant can assure her of the solidity of God's promise for a return to normal life in Judah, when the dispersion is passed and God recalls the people to the land that was given to their ancestors.

This must mean for us today that it is not sufficient for churches to criticize the militarization of U.S. foreign policy and its powerful financial and military backing for world institutions (the World Trade Organization, International Monetary Fund, and World Bank) to "guarantee" U.S.-style free trade. Criticism such as the antiglobalization demonstrations in Seattle, Quebec, and Genoa is necessary and important, but it is not sufficient. Along with Christians from the whole world, we must begin dreaming of alternative structures to govern a just world with real freedom and justice for all. In part, this is a matter of strengthening existing institutions like the United Nations, the World Court, and the International Labor Council. But we also need to imagine alternatives, especially in business organizations. We have been taught to sacrifice democracy to "efficiency," which allows defenders of the current system to disregard claims by workers and honor only the constraints of the Market. Surely, we need an economic system where both constraints are given due respect.

PART D'

Rejection of God's Word and Prophet
(Jeremiah 34—38)

The five chapters we are about to examine all have one subject, the word of God and its mostly negative reception. In all, the prophet is the messenger for God. But each chapter is a separate story, and they evidently have different origins, with no reason to suspect a common author or authors. Some would see chapter 37 as the beginning of a chronicle by Baruch, but that is sheer speculation.

Within the overall structure of the book of Jeremiah, these chapters on the word and its reception correspond to chapters 7—10, on the same general subject, in the first half of the book. This does not mean that these stories were composed as a counterpart to 7—10; that they were not is suggested by the fact that in the LXX, which does not share the ring structure of MT, they appear in a different location (in LXX, they are chapters 41—45). Nevertheless, it does appear that the final editors of MT Jeremiah intended for Jeremiah 34—38 to balance Jeremiah 7—10.

These chapters are all prose narratives with Jeremiah as the protagonist. Their order, which is the same in MT and LXX, is not chronological. The arrangement appears to be topical, focused on the word of God and its (negative) reception by the people of Jerusalem and Judah.

Two Case Studies in a Stiff-necked People (Jeremiah 34 and 35)

Chapter 34 centers on the release of debt slaves according to the provisions of Deuteronomy 15 and the failure of Jerusalem's people to honor the law and their pledges, while chapter 35 contrasts the negative attitude of the people toward the commands of God with the positive obedience of the descendants of Jonadab ben Rechab to the orders of their forefather. The verdict against the people is negative in both cases, although the sons of Jonadab come off well in chapter 35.

Release from debts (Jeremiah 34). Verses 1–7 of this chapter provide the setting for the incident related later: Jerusalem in the days of Zedekiah during the final siege of the city by the Babylonian army in 587–586 B.C.E. The word of God for King Zedekiah has two sides. On the one hand, the city will be delivered to the Babylonians, and Zedekiah will fall into their hands, forced to deal with Nebuchadnezzar face to face. On the other hand, he is assured that he will die in peace and receive burial honors, apparently in Babylon. This promise seems to contradict the threat against Zedekiah and his people in Jeremiah 21:1–10. The report in 1 Kings 25:5–7 says that Zedekiah was captured and taken to Nebuchadnezzar in Riblah, where his sons were slaughtered before his eyes; then his eyes were put out, and he was put in chains and dragged off to Babylon. There seems to be no way of reconciling all of this with the promise in Jeremiah 34:5. None of the other texts offer an option of being taken to Babylon in peace and with honor. Babylon is the empire, and it will not tolerate a minor king who refuses to submit. This is the way of empire in all times in human history. Think of the way in which Iraq was dealt with, first in 1991 and then again in 2003, and also Afghanistan, for refusing to obey the commands of the mighty ones. In the context of Jeremiah 34, the point seems to be that God is more interested in punishing the people than in punishing their king, quite contrary to the usual logic of the Bible in making kings responsible for the fate of their peoples.

The central story of the chapter begins in Jeremiah 34:8. The issue is debt slavery, the only kind of slavery that existed among Israelites according to their law. If a debtor was unable to pay what he owed, his creditor could require the slavery of the debtor or any member of his family. There was a limit, however. Such debt slavery could not exceed six years, so that the seventh was a year of freedom (Deut. 15:1–6). Both Deuteronomy and Jeremiah 34:14 relate this release to God's release of the Hebrew slaves at the time of the exodus. As descendants of slaves released by God, the Israelites are told not to submit their brothers and sisters to harsh slavery. Now we hear that Zedekiah made a covenant with the (wealthy) people of Jerusalem to give release (*deror*) to their debt slaves. In effect, this meant that old debts would no longer be collected, since the slaves were paying off their old debts with their labor. Nothing is said about motivation. Perhaps the covenanters hoped to placate God and gain relief from the besieging Babylonian army.

Verses 15 and 16 both begin with the verb *shuv*, turn. "You turned and did what was right in my eyes" (Jer. 34:15), and then "you turned and profaned my name, each one taking back your male slave and your female slave whom you had released" (34:16). "Now, since you did not grant *deror* (release), each to your neighbor, therefore I will grant *deror* to the sword, to pestilence and to famine," says God (34:17). As the reader can see, the punishment neatly fits the crime.

Verses 18–19 are confusing. The calf that was cut in two reminds us of Genesis 15, where God's flame passes through the two halves of a young heifer Abraham has prepared in order to assure the covenant they have just established. This Abraham text is the only place in the Bible where this curious practice is specifically mentioned, although the expression for making a covenant in Hebrew means literally to "cut" a covenant, perhaps an allusion to this kind of ceremony. In Jeremiah, God says that the covenant-breakers will be cut the way the calf was cut. But the syntax of Jeremiah 34:19 with regard to the calf is not clear. Translators must doctor it a bit to make sense of it for readers. The cutting of the calf is not even mentioned in LXX. Its statement, "the ox that I gave to be worked by him" is, in context, unintelligible, so perhaps the Greek translators understood the Hebrew text no better than their modern counterparts.

The upshot of this lack of pity for the poor in Jerusalem will be that God will send the Babylonian army back to destroy the city, burn it, and turn Judah into a desolation. The whole incident leads us to reflect on the conflict between morality and profit, a very contemporary issue and evidently one equally important in sixth-century Palestine. The appeal to God's release of the ancestors from their slavery in Egypt is an appeal to conscience. But it conflicts with profit. To release debt slaves means to accept a loss that will not be recovered. In ancient Israel, the Sinaitic law had enshrined the concern for the poor so that when the creditor failed to fulfill obligations in this sense, the censure would be unanimous. This did not assure that a creditor would act against private interest for the well-being of the poor, but at least the moral obligation was clear and universally accepted. The issues are fudged today. Business rules, which have been foisted onto general society, affirm that each must act for his or her own profit. A naïve faith is proclaimed that should this be done by all, that the consequent benefit for those who have most capital will somehow trickle down to benefit the rest, including the poorest members of society. In spite of much evidence to the contrary, such as the disastrous effects of privatizing energy in California, the value of private profit taking is an article of faith in our society and cannot be questioned without seeming unpatriotic. Regardless of the difference in societal norms between ancient Israel and the contemporary U.S.A., the issue of the conflict between the well-being of the poor and the profits of the wealthy is the same. Jeremiah takes a stand for the well-being of the poor in our chapter.

There is another point in Jeremiah 34 that must not escape our attention. God is going to bring the Babylonian army back against Jerusalem and Judah. In other words, empire is not always alien to God's will. On occasion, God uses empire as for God's governance of the world, and the will of God in these cases is that we submit to empire. This is even more apparent with the dynamics of today's empire than with the Babylonian one. Empires always rest ultimately on military superiority at any time in history. But empires can have legitimate justifications as well, such as the peace that the Romans offered and to a large extent delivered, the Christian faith that the Spanish empire offered and often delivered, and the democracy that the U.S. empire promises and to some extent delivers. (We won't explore the free market, which this empire always imposes and whose value for subordinate peoples is much more doubtful than that of democracy.) Empire is not for Jeremiah always evil, in spite of its reliance on military might. In our explorations of this remarkable prophetic book, we should not lose sight of this matter. In the history of Israel, the Babylonian empire—symbol of proud military might in both testaments of the Bible—can, nevertheless, at times be the instrument of God to straighten out God's people. There might also be times when submission to the U.S. empire is God's will for one or another people on this troubled globe.

An obedient people (Jeremiah 35). Jeremiah has just condemned the leaders of the city to exile and destruction, because under King Zedekiah they have refused to fulfill God's demands in the law. Now, in this chapter, we are given an incident that took place much earlier, during the reign of King Jehoiakim, that bears on a people who are remarkable for their obedience, the descendants of Jonadab son of Rechab. The apparent reason for this flagrant violation of chronology (from Zedekiah's time back to that of Jehoiakim) is to have contrary case studies in obedience or lack thereof. The Rechabites, a strange group that we would call a primitivist sect, are cited as a positive example to the Judahites. It must have seemed strange to most inhabitants of Jerusalem for the prophet to take this sectarian group as a model. But the point is a specific one—obedience—and, on this point, they are an exemplary case.

These people refuse to grow grain or vineyards, and they refuse to build houses for themselves. Evidently, they live in portable tents and make their living pasturing flocks. Of course, there have been from time immemorial people in Palestine who live in such a style. The ancestors in Genesis are pictured as this sort of people. What is strange is that these Rechabites live this lifestyle as a matter of principle and reject the urban life of Jerusalem, at least for themselves and their children. By doing so, they raise uncomfortable questions about the inhabitants of Jerusalem, who surround themselves with urban comforts, modest by twenty-first century standards, but surely perceived then as greatly superior to the primitive lifestyle of the Rechabites. This countercultural group had taken temporary refuge in the midst of the city because of the Babylonian threat (Jer. 35:11). It was for this reason that Jeremiah was able to encounter them and take them to the temple for his experiment. He was going to prove to the Jerusalemites that it was possible to be obedient even when obedience was uncomfortable or unpleasant, as it surely was for the Rechabites. Not to drink wine and not to eat bread and not to live in houses, with the privacy and security these offered, was not an attractive lifestyle. But to do so on principle and not just because of need must have seemed an incomprehensible hardheadedness to most Jerusalemites. The reason given by the Rechabites was, quite simply, Our father Jonadab ordered us to live in this manner (35:6–7). That settled the question for them!

Jeremiah found this faithfulness to the father Jonadab admirable, in contrast to the Jerusalemites' lack of obedience to the word of God (35:14–15). We would expect the word that requires obedience to be the Torah, the Sinaitic law revealed to Moses that expressed the will of God for the people God had just rescued from Egyptian slavery. But in this chapter, as in many others, Jeremiah is also concerned about obedience to the words of God's prophets. Evidently, the specific word Jeremiah has in mind is his insistent demand that the people of Judah, the inhabitants of Jerusalem, and their kings submit voluntarily to the king of Babylon (the same word quoted by Zedekiah in Jer. 34:2–5). All the judgments that God has announced through the prophet are going to be brought on Jerusalem and Judah because they have refused to listen and obey, unlike these odd Rechabites who persist in keeping the commands of their forefather. This is the real message of this chapter, as it was of chapter 34.

The chapter ends with a brief oracle for the Rechabites (35:18–19). It promises that there will forever be a descendant of theirs to "stand before me." This oracle of promise seems to parody the promise to David that there will always be one of his descendants to sit on his throne in Jerusalem (2 Sam. 7:13–16; Ps. 89:27–29). This promise was the religious foundation for the royal family in Jerusalem. The dominant tradition in the book of Jeremiah challenges it (see Jer. 22:1–30), although there are a few sayings that agree with it (see Jer. 33:19–22). The parody here reflects the dominant tradition, which does not support the Davidic line.

Jeremiah does not comment on the Rechabite lifestyle as such, just the obedience that it reflects. Nevertheless, his use of these outsiders as a model to teach the people of Jerusalem reflects some critical distance from the dominant lifestyle in the city. The mere existence of such groups would suggest a different view of the lifestyle that people in the city took for granted. This is always a healthy role for groups like the hippies or other communities who hold all things in common among themselves. But the emphasis of this chapter rests on the fidelity of these people to the vow taken by the ancestor.

A King Versus a Scroll (Jeremiah 36:1–32)

In Jeremiah 36, for the first time, a book (scroll) takes the place of the physical presence of the prophet as the deliverer of God's word. It is the beginning of scripture. Through the story of the scroll, it becomes clear that the issue is not the political conflict between public personae, king and prophet, but the presence of the word of God, with or without a body to deliver it. There is a correct response to God's word and an incorrect one, and it is not an issue of whether one likes or dislikes the person who bears it. The word when it becomes a book takes on a role of its own, independent of the human figure who wrote it.

This is a chapter highly charged with political passions. Such passions are part of human life and should not be denied or concealed. The two poles in this drama are Jeremiah, Baruch the scribe, and their scroll, on the one side, and the king, Jehoiakim, the scroll-destroyer on the other. In the middle stand the scribes, government bureaucrats whose role is more difficult to discern, precisely because they are accomplished experts in concealing their inner feelings and political intentions. Their survival depends on keeping the favor of the king, and so they have learned not to let their opinions appear on the surface. But a careful reading of this text will allow us to make likely judgments about the veiled intentions of these cautious persons.

The narrative begins by setting the scene (Jer. 36:1–8). It is the fourth year of Jehoiakim, a fateful year in which Nebuchadnezzar establishes his dominance over the known world by defeating the Egyptians at Carchemish. For the rest of the lives of King Jehoiakim and Jeremiah, Babylon will be *the* imperial power, with unchallenged military might in the entire region. The politics of all the kingdoms of the known world will be determined by how they respond to Babylonian rule. If favorably, they survive; if unfavorably, they face invasion and certain defeat. From this year on,

Babylonian power cannot be successfully challenged, and any attempt to do so will be foolhardy. So, it is a critical year. Egypt is removed from the scene as a possible balance to Babylonian power. Jeremiah and his sidekick Baruch represent the political position that submission to Babylon is not only politically expedient, which must have been the prevailing opinion among wise counselors in the kingdom, but also theologically correct. It is the will of God that all nations, and Judah first of all, submit to this new empire. Much of the material concerning Jeremiah's conflicts with his relatives in Anathoth, the priests of Jerusalem, and other prophets must have been driven by opposition to the theological position represented by Jeremiah. In the days of a particular empire, it is a pretty universal opinion that submission is the only prudent course of action, since resistance is tantamount to political suicide. But it is quite another matter to hold that submission is the "will of God," that is, that it is the *right* thing to do at this difficult moment. There will be many who call for a passive resistance, a preparation for better days when changed military circumstances make open resistance a practical course. But Jeremiah and Baruch are saying more. They believe that submission to Babylon is the will of God, and any other course of action is disobedience to the word of God. This has been reiterated many times in earlier chapters of the book and is presumably the content of the scroll that Jeremiah dictates to Baruch.

Baruch picks a time when crowds will be present in the temple to read the scroll he has written from Jeremiah's dictation. It is the ninth month of the fifth year (LXX says the ninth month of the eighth year), on a day of fasting. The reading is performed in the chambers of Gemariah, one of the sons of Shaphan, a famous scribe in the court of Josiah (2 Kings 22—23). Ahikam, another son of Shaphan, protected Jeremiah from the murderous intent of the temple personnel in one of the first years of Jehoiakim, according to Jeremiah 26:24, and later we learn that Gedaliah, son of Ahikam and grandson of Shaphan, will be, as the Babylonian governor, Jeremiah's protector at Mizpah (Jer. 40). So we can presume that Gemariah also is sympathetic to Jeremiah and the political stance he advocates.

Micaiah, the son of Gemariah, is impressed with the reading and proceeds to the king's house to a gathering of high officials (Jer. 36:12). The officials gathered in these chambers are influential persons in the royal court, for it does not seem necessary or appropriate to pose such political positions to the people at large. Micaiah reports the contents of Baruch's scroll, which are evidently considered a very serious matter that deserves consideration at the highest levels of government. Baruch is called for a second reading to these royal officials (36:14–15), which he proceeds to perform. The reaction in verses 17–19 is revealing. First, the officials ask about the origins of this remarkable document. Baruch answers that Jeremiah has dictated its contents. Note that neither Baruch nor the officials ask about the divine source; they just want to establish human responsibility, a matter that concerns them as political figures. The theological authority of this document is not something they can assess. But they do know that this document is explosive material that will fall like a bombshell on the king's ears. So, they recommend that both Jeremiah and Baruch hide in some place that the officials do not wish to know.

They must now present this important matter to the king for his consideration. They know it will provoke the anger of the king, so it is best that they read it themselves, letting Baruch take refuge in a hidden location. Are the officials of the same opinion as Baruch's scroll? Bureaucrats that they are, they do not make their opinions known. But the importance they give to the document and the precautions they take to protect Jeremiah and Baruch suggest that they share to some extent the opinions just read to them. When the king is inclining toward resisting the empire, it is a little surprising to find his high officials taking a pro-Babylonian stance, if, indeed, we interpret them correctly. It is, of course, not surprising that they seek to moderate the king's inclinations toward confrontation, when they know full well that confrontation can only end in disaster. But the scroll goes further than that in making submission a matter of God's will. We can suppose that the officials are hiding their own convictions behind the scroll, which represents similar views in a safe manner—safe for the officials, that is. They are, then, doing nothing more than informing the king of an important opinion among his subjects.

But of course, the book of Jeremiah is not interested in the opinions of the scribes so much as in their fidelity in transmitting the word of God to confront the king. It is he who must make the decision with respect to that word. And the king's response leaves no doubt about his political position and his scorn for theological opinions that undergird contrary political opinions. As the scroll is read, the king takes the pages that have been read, cuts them with a knife, and throws the cut strips into the fire he has in his winter house to keep warm. And, comments the narrator, he and his servants did not rend their garments (Jer. 36:24). This is an obvious reference to a similar situation narrated in 2 Kings 22, where it is said that Josiah, Jehoiakim's father, tore his garments when he heard the reading of the scroll that was found in the temple. In Jeremiah 22:13–17, Jeremiah makes a similarly unfavorable comparison between these two kings concerning the justice of their actions. Here, the matter at issue is their respect and obedience to the word of God. Again, Jehoiakim is exposed as the bad example to his father's good example. As the officials expected, the king orders the arrest of Jeremiah and Baruch, but, comments the narrator, God hid them (Jer. 36:26, an MT editorial improvement; God is not mentioned in this context in LXX).

The remainder of chapter 36 (verses 27–32) reaffirms the judgment on Jehoiakim and Jerusalem that was contained in the scroll, and God orders Jeremiah to dictate a new scroll with the same sayings and others of a similar sort to complete the judgment. The actions of Jehoiakim merit a special divine decision regarding the stripping of royal dignity that will surround his death and the lack of a successor on the throne (36:30–31). The word is to be recorded in a book where it will be preserved for future generations to consult and to confirm the insolence of the royal scorn for that word.

The relations between religion and politics are indeed complex. When Jeremiah and Hananiah advocated competing positions before King Zedekiah, who was to decide which one truly represented the word of God? The political stakes were high and evoked passion, thus the scorn with which Jehoiakim treated the scroll. This was a politician's response to an open defiance of his political plans. One would expect nothing else. Probably, Jehoiakim supported his policies with religious expressions of piety about how God could do wonders to defend God's favored people. It is impossible to separate politics from religion or religion from politics in times of crisis and high emotion. Jeremiah seems in retrospect to have faithfully represented the word of the true God, but it would surely have been difficult to be sure at the time, as it is today, to judge between conflicting political opinions that claim God's support. One thinks of the Crusades in the European Middle Ages, where both Christians and Muslims acted in full confidence that they defended God's cause.

The Word of God, the Prophet, the King, and the Officials (Jeremiah 37—38)

Although the narrative in these two chapters is a continuation of the theme of the rejection of the word of God, it is also part of a new section, Jeremiah 37—43, often called the passion of Jeremiah. This is a third-person narrative about the trials of Jeremiah surrounding the capture and destruction of Jerusalem. To it are appended a long section of preaching to the Judean refugees in Egypt (Jer. 44) and a private oracle to Baruch (Jer. 45). The great Norwegian scholar Sigmund Mowinckel, in his classic 1914 study of the composition of Jeremiah, assigned these chapters to what he called the B-corpus of narratives about Jeremiah, while he assigned Jeremiah 34 and 35 to a sermonic composition that he labelled the C-corpus. He believed they were composed at different times, though the language of both is Deuteronomistic (Deuteronomy-like). I accept this analysis with regard to sources and compositional history, but, in this commentary, I am analyzing the present structure and message of the book. As we have seen, in its last stage of composition in the tradition leading to MT, after the LXX translation had been made, the book of Jeremiah was formed into a vaguely ring-shaped structure. This version of the book reflects theological concerns of the Judean leaders who were building the Yehud province under Persian authorities. Out of the materials of the Jeremiah tradition, they shaped a Jeremiah figure who responded to their theological needs. And for this purpose, chapters 37—38 belong with chapters 34—36, for all of them deal with the single-minded preaching of Jeremiah announcing the coming destruction of the city by the Babylonian empire and with the rejection of that message by the public authorities in different moments of the twenty-year period leading up to the destruction.

Chapters 37—38 are set in the final years of Zedekiah during the siege of Jerusalem. As we have observed before, chronology is not a matter of great concern to the organizers of this book, though they preserved the chronological labels in the tradition. During a hopeful break in the siege when the Egyptian army shows up on the scene, God gives Jeremiah a message for the king: don't get your hopes up. The Babylonian army will be back shortly, and they will take the city and burn it with fire (Jer. 37:8–10). It is the same old message the prophet has been repeating on every occasion. He is convinced that Babylonian control of Judah is God's will, so no political strategy has any hope of altering the negative outcome. It is important for us today to realize that religion is not just a private feeling, something that has no bearing on public policy. Modernity would have us believe that this is so. It is possible, say its spokespersons, for families of totally different beliefs to live side by side in peace and not even have to negotiate their differences. Toleration in religious beliefs is possible as long as one keeps one's religion to oneself and one's family. This is, of course, not Jeremiah's understanding of God's presence and action in Israel's national life.

In chapter 36, King Jehoiakim was ultimately responsible for the country's rejection of God's word. There, the scribes and high officials of the kingdom were more receptive to the theological and political message of Jeremiah and Baruch than was the king. These roles are reversed in Jeremiah 37—38. The officials are aggressive in punishing Jeremiah for treason when he utters discouraging words. King Zedekiah, by contrast, is anxious to seek out the prophet for a view of his situation different from that of his officials. The king and Jeremiah meet in secret and privately arrange to protect the prophet. Thus, while Jeremiah is independent and speaks his word from God unaffected by friendship or enmity in his hearers, he is willing to compromise when the message is not affected but his personal security is involved. We have no way of knowing how historically accurate this narrative is.

Jeremiah 37:1–10 sets the scene for what will follow in chapters 37— 38. The Babylonian army is besieging the city, which is now ruled by Zedekiah, one of Josiah's sons. Unexpectedly, some relief has come from the appearance of the Egyptian army, which prompts a withdrawal by the Babylonians. In these circumstances, Zedekiah sends for Jeremiah and asks that he pray to the Holy One "for us." Jeremiah, who is "not yet" in prison, responds not with prayer but with a judgment oracle, the same message he has been delivering for twenty years. God will deliver the city and its king into the hands of Babylon. In some of his previous oracles, he had mentioned the possibility of escape, should there be a radical departure from evil ways. Now, he says there is no hope of escape. The withdrawal of the Babylonians means nothing; they will be back. Ultimately, this is not a political analysis but a theological one. God wills to turn Jerusalem and its king over to Nebuchadnezzar, so the tactical moves of the armies mean nothing. Poor Zedekiah! His hopes for a change on the part of the Holy One are, according to Jeremiah, mere illusions.

In Jeremiah 37:11–16, focus shifts from Jeremiah's message to the person Jeremiah. He wishes to take advantage of the respite offered by Babylonian withdrawal to return to his hometown, perhaps to look after the property we heard about in chapter 32. Not surprisingly, he is detained at the gate and accused of going over to the Babylonians. The sentinel in charge of the gate understands that Jeremiah is a traitor, and "the officials" beat him and throw him into prison.

Jeremiah 37:17–21 returns to the main theme of these chapters, the word of God and its rejection. The king, Zedekiah, sends for Jeremiah, who is brought to the palace. Now, the request is not for prayer but for the word of God. Evidently, the king hopes for a new word, something different from the repetitive drone Jeremiah has pronounced until now about delivery to Babylon. The narrator makes Jeremiah offer a brief hope in the first exchange: "Is there any word from the Holy One?" "There is." But it turns out to mean nothing. The word is, "You shall be handed over to the king of Babylon." Now, surprisingly, Jeremiah has a personal petition to make of the king. The king wanted an independent opinion, and Jeremiah gave it to him. His lackeys were saying that nothing would happen, but look at what is happening. Is it wrong to speak the truth? "You," that is Zedekiah and his officials, have imprisoned Jeremiah in conditions where he will surely die. Here, Jeremiah holds the king responsible for the actions of his officials. The CEO is where the buck stops, and, in the kingdom of Judah, that is Zedekiah. Evidently, Jeremiah did not misjudge Zedekiah's sentiments, for the king now orders a softening of the conditions of imprisonment and a guarantee of minimum food rations while they last—surprising concessions coming from a condemned king!

In Jeremiah 38:1–6, however, the king vacillates again. In a meeting, his officials pose their objections to Jeremiah and request the death penalty. "This man must die, for he is weakening the hands of the army...He does not seek the welfare of the people" (38:4). It is not a false accusation. Jeremiah, in calling on the people to go over to the Babylonians to save their lives (Jer. 21:9), is committing treason, and in a country at war, treason merits the death penalty. Zedekiah's answer reminds us of the gospels' picture of Pilate during Jesus' trial: "He is in your hands" (Jer. 38:5; Mt. 27). The MT strengthens this judgment with an addition, "the king is powerless against you," a rather surprising admission. The officials have Jeremiah thrown into a pit with no water but only mud, the very image of Sheol, the realm of the dead. They suppose he will die there of hunger and thirst.

In another aside (Jer. 38:7–13), a new character appears in a small scene that has to do with Jeremiah's survival rather than the word of God. The new person is Ebed-Melech, an Ethiopian eunuch in the king's household (the fact that he is a eunuch was added in MT as a colorful detail that enhances the story). On his own initiative, this eunuch approaches the king on behalf of the prophet. "These men" have acted wickedly in putting Jeremiah where he will surely die. The king assigns thirty men to assist Ebed-Melech in a rescue operation, which is then described in detail.

By Jeremiah 38:14, we are back to the main story. The king again sends for Jeremiah. They meet at one of the side entrances to the temple courtyard, which apparently means that Jeremiah is no longer a prisoner. Again, the king wants to consult Jeremiah who is, naturally, suspicious. He has given his message many times and has no intention of changing it. Jeremiah accuses the king of wanting to kill him if he tells the truth, which the king denies with a "secret oath" (the secrecy is another juicy detail added by MT in the final revision). He will not kill Jeremiah nor turn him over to "these men" (MT adds, "who seek your life"). Such an oath, of course, made in secret, means little since nobody can verify it if not fulfilled, not even the prophet, who in that case would be dead.

Jeremiah offers the king one way out, to turn himself over to the Babylonians. If he does, he will live and the city will be spared. But Zedekiah is less afraid of the Babylonians than of the Judeans who surrendered earlier; they will kill him. Jeremiah assures him that the Holy One says his life will be spared. (Now, it is the king's turn to be asked to trust with no guarantee.) If he insists on sticking it out and defending the city, it will fall, and the women will mock him. There ends the message, and the assumption is that again the king does not "listen" (that is, obey), because he is too weak a person for so drastic an action.

The incident closes with a little agreement between Zedekiah and Jeremiah, who end up being partners, at least in this small measure (Jer. 38:24–28). The king proposes that Jeremiah give a false version if asked about the conversation, and Jeremiah agrees. Evidently, Zedekiah fears his officers and wishes well to Jeremiah, though not enough to publicly confront his subordinates. Jeremiah's agreement shows that he is not ready to be a martyr unnecessarily. His obligation to God is to deliver the word to its designated recipients, not to sacrifice his life for the cause of strict truth.

This text models how a servant of God is to act. The servant must be faithful to the truth of the divine message under all circumstances, even at the cost of liberty and perhaps life. The word of God is nonnegotiable, and Jeremiah sticks to it regardless of the circumstances. That word runs against popular opinion and the government's official policies. Christians today must take this very seriously. If they live in a country like the U.S. that uses military might as a tool for its policy objectives around the globe, there will be many occasions when one who represents God's word will be called upon to confront that government's policies. This is not negotiable. But in matters of survival, the prophet has a certain amount of flexibility, as long as the word itself is not compromised. An interesting object lesson!

PART C'

Invasion from the North Accomplished
(Jeremiah 39—45)

Early in the book of Jeremiah, we encountered sections dealing with the broken marriage between the Holy One and Israel (Jer. 2—3) and the threat of the enemy from the north (Jer. 4—6). Now, as we move outward from the center of the book's ring structure, we encounter actualization of the threat from the north (Jer. 39—43) and a further reflection on the causes for the rupture between the Holy One and Israel (Jer. 44). Jeremiah 45 is a comment directed to the scribe who has written down Jeremiah's prophecies, Baruch, the son of Neriah.

The City Is Taken and Destroyed (Jeremiah 39)

Much of this chapter is an "objective" account of the taking and destruction of Jerusalem, with no reference to Jeremiah and no moralistic or theological comment. The precise dates of the siege are given, indicating a span of some eighteen months between the arrival of the Babylonians in the tenth month of the ninth year and the fourth month of the eleventh year of Zedekiah, when the walls were breached and the city entered. Babylonian headquarters were set up at the middle gate. The Babylonian generals are listed, but their king, called Nebuchadrezzar here, seems to be absent. We shall learn a little later that his headquarters are at Riblah in the area of Hamath to the north. He is directing the military actions but has no reason to follow the secondary campaign to Jerusalem. He stays closer to the main action in Syria to the north. The account tells of the destruction of Jerusalem by the Babylonian army and the savage revenge that Nebuchadrezzar takes on Zedekiah, killing his sons before his eyes in Riblah, then blinding him and taking him to Babylon to live in ignominy in that center of empire.

The events narrated are not new information to the reader of the Bible, since 2 Kings 25 tells the same story. But here in the book of Jeremiah, they have a special significance: They show that the word of God delivered repeatedly by the prophet was, in fact, realized. Since Zedekiah and the inhabitants of Jerusalem persisted in resisting the Babylonians, the city was destroyed and the king reduced to a blind parody of himself. Without any comment from the editors, the reader is allowed to draw the obvious conclusion, that the word of God makes reality and that Jeremiah was speaking the truth about that word.

In Jeremiah 39:11, our story returns to the fate of the prophet Jeremiah, bearer of the word of God that is now producing its effects in the destruction of Jerusalem. The military commanders search out Jeremiah in his prison and entrust him to Gedaliah, the grandson of Shaphan, to whom they have committed the governing of the province. The text pointedly tells us that Jeremiah "dwelt in the midst of the people" (39:14). A little later, our text will return to this same moment and treat it in a slightly different manner (Jer. 40:1–6). Here, we hear that Gedaliah is given charge of Jeremiah "in order to take him home" (39:14). Jeremiah is not consulted, but evidently the imperial army wishes him well. Babylonian intelligence has apparently informed these officers that Jeremiah is not part of the problem and can be treated respectfully, quite contrary to the treatment of others. Perhaps they believe that Jeremiah is a deserter, as did the Judahite guards at the gate who captured him in the first place (Jer. 37:13). But this turns out not to be true, since Jeremiah is perfectly content to "dwell in the midst of the people."

It is evident from their treatment of the king and the city that the Babylonians do not intend to destroy Judah. We will learn later (Jer. 52:29) that in this round only 832 persons were deported. Meanwhile, lands were granted to the poor so that they might cultivate them. Gedaliah, a high Judahite official, is appointed to be responsible for the province (see also Jer. 40:5). So what was the objective of all the impressive show of military strength if the land was left more or less as it was? The very harsh treatment meted out to Zedekiah shows that the goal was to cut off the Davidic royal administration, which the Babylonians perceived as contrary to imperial interests. We might compare it with today's interventions in Iraq to get rid of Saddam Hussein, in Yugoslavia to remove Slovodan Milosevic, and in Afghanistan to remove the Taliban government, all seen as inimical to imperial interests. Empires do not always wish to destroy all local initiative, but they do not tolerate governments that they perceive as hostile to their interests.

Interestingly, Jeremiah 39:4–13 is not yet present in the LXX version of the book. Even though MT does not add information to what we learn from 2 Kings 25, it does direct our attention to the fate of the common people and not just the fate of the prophet who bears God's word. This seems a correct decision. God is not just concerned with kings and ministers of religion but with the fate of peoples and nations. We, as people who wish to be faithful to God, must also keep a broad perspective and not allow our "religious" understanding to exclude matters that are of great concern to the lives of ordinary people and hence to God.

At the end of the chapter, verses 15–18 interrupt the story about Jeremiah to return briefly to Ebed-Melech, the Ethiopian who engineered the prophet's release from the pit into which the officials had thrown him (Jer. 38:11–13). It is evidently a sort of flashback, since Jeremiah is again in the prison from which we have just been informed the officers of the Babylonian army had freed him. The oracle for Ebed-Melech has two parts: a repeat of the frequent threat of the destruction of the city and a promise of salvation for Ebed-Melech, who will not be given into the hands of those he fears (either the Babylonians or perhaps the officials of the king whose aims he had frustrated). The point of this brief paragraph is that obedience to God's word gets very concrete rewards, even when the city is collapsing due to the disobedience of the king and his officials.

Judah Set Up as a Babylonian Province (Jeremiah 40:1–12)

Our story now gets back to Jeremiah who, it turns out, had been in the crowd of nobles who were being taken to Babylon (the 832). The head of the military unit leading the people spots Jeremiah and deals with him individually. This soldier is very familiar with the word of God that Jeremiah has been delivering; in fact, he recites the message quite faithfully in Jeremiah 40:2–3. He recognizes in Jeremiah a friend of Babylon and so offers him special treatment. The first and "best" offer is the possibility of coming to Babylon and receiving special treatment at the hands of the government there. But if Jeremiah prefers, he may return to the land and establish himself among his own people in the province the Babylonians are founding.

Jeremiah does not hesitate in choosing the latter course. This shows he is not really a friend of Babylon; he is just convinced that this is the day of this empire and that God wills it so. Politically, Jeremiah sympathizes with the province being set up under Babylonian protection and commissioned to Gedaliah, one of the grandsons of Shaphan, with whose family Jeremiah has maintained friendly relations for some time. In the complex politics of the day, Jeremiah has decided against the Davidic royal house in both its expressions (Jehoiachin and Zedekiah) and favored a more modest project that accepts Babylonian hegemony.

Gedaliah is presented in Jeremiah 40:7–12 as a man of peace who wishes to draw together the wounded people of Judah and motivate them to work and prosper without any pretensions of national glory. He promises to represent their interests before the Babylonian authorities who trust in him (rather than serving as a channel for Babylonian interests in Judah). It is a difficult course of action, and he never gets to carry it out because hotheaded nationalists among the Judahites are already planning his murder. So, we cannot know how successful he would have been. Jeremiah was convinced this was God's will and no doubt believed that God would make it possible. But there was no miracle forthcoming to protect Gedaliah's life.

Evidently, there are times when empire is part of God's plan for the earth and its peoples. Jeremiah was convinced that his was such a time. This does not necessarily mean that today is such a time, but it might be so. Maybe in God's governance God wills the current domination of the U.S. empire over much of the world. For Christians living within the U.S. and benefitting from the imposition of the dollar standard on the whole world, this is, of course, a very comfortable position—which ought to make us suspicious. For Jeremiah, Babylonian hegemony may have been the will of God, but it was anything but comfortable. It put him at odds with his family and his friends and put him in jail. We are led to believe that this is the normal fate of God's prophets, so when a prophet says, "Peace, peace," we should be very suspicious (Jer. 28). But the imperial option does remain an open one.

A Political Purist Destroys a Viable Project
(Jeremiah 40:13—41:18)

Jeremiah again disappears from the scene while the text concentrates on political developments. The course of power, that is, politics, has its own autonomy, though it is also where God's projects come to pass or are frustrated. By now, the reader of Jeremiah has been guided to understand that God's project is to subdue all the nations to the Babylonian empire (Jer. 27) until the time comes when Babylon, too, will have to drink the cup of the wrath of the Holy One (Jer. 25:12–16). As the story has unfolded, we have been led to believe that a provincial government for Judah under Gedaliah, a Judahite scribe, is God's chosen project. Our hero Jeremiah, after denouncing all other political projects, has embraced this one. His support for Gedaliah's puppet regime stands in sharp contrast to his denouncing kings Jehoiakim, Jehoiachin, and Zedekiah, and even his implicit critique of the "good king" Josiah for having led a false conversion (Jer. 3:6–13). All of those projects fell under the condemnation of God and God's prophet. Now, finally, a political project appears with which Jeremiah feels comfortable.

But the project is shattered by a despicable scoundrel named Ishmael son of Nethaniah. This man is of royal lineage (Jer. 41:1), and he has taken refuge in Ammon across the Jordan River from Judah. He enters our story when Johanan son of Kareah, one of Gedaliah's armed supporters, accuses Ishmael of plotting murder against the governor (Jer. 40:13–16). Like any armed force, Johanan's troop has its sources of intelligence, which in military parlance means knowledge of the enemies' plans, and he has learned of this plot. Not only does he report to Gedaliah what he knows, but he also proposes to nip the problem in the bud with a carefully planned secret assassination of Ishmael. Gedaliah's peaceful nature is revealed when he refuses to believe Johanan and forbids the political murder.

Jeremiah 41:1–10 tells how the royal scoundrel Ishmael, with no moral sense at all, comes with ten armed companions to Gedaliah at his quarters in Mizpah. They are received with a dinner, and, after having dined, they murder their host Gedaliah "because the king of Babylon had appointed him governor in the land" (41:2). Ishmael is a purist who wants no truck with the empire. He kills not only Gedaliah, but also the Judahite persons surrounding him and the Babylonian soldiers assigned to him. There is now no room for reconciliation with the Babylonian power. Being of royal blood, Ishmael no doubt hopes to gain power in an independent kingdom, should he succeed in establishing one. He may even realize that this will not be possible. Some politicians prefer to die for their cause rather than make concessions that will render the cause at least partially viable. Of such a sort was Ishmael.

In an important sense, the story could end here. With the death of Gedaliah and the provocation of the empire, the Babylonian experiment with autonomous provincial government is over. Now, there is no turning back from straightforward subjugation to Babylon. But before returning to Jeremiah, our story deepens its plot. This book has been written and edited by supporters of a later Persian provincial government, and they want to make clear the folly of openly confronting an empire that is vastly superior in military might. Jeremiah is a good figure for their case, because with this prophet they can also contend that God wills submission to the empire—the Babylonians in Jeremiah's day and, by implication, the Persians in a later day. So the story continues.

Ishmael, the nationalist purist, is presented as thoroughly despicable. Having assassinated the governor and the military contingent at Mizpah, he now lays a plot for some innocent pilgrims who are bringing offerings to the temple of the Holy One (41:5). Ishmael, as representative of the royal line, goes to meet the eighty pilgrims. He entices them into the city in the name of Gedaliah, whom he has just murdered (a fact unknown to the pilgrims). Then, he slaughters them and throws their bodies into a large cistern in the city. Ten of them, however, when they see the fate that has befallen them, offer an enticement of produce of the land in exchange for their lives, a deal that the merciless Ishmael accepts.

The story then returns to Johanan, who had discovered Ishmael's intentions and offered to stop him with a prudential murder. When he learns of what Ishmael has done, he gets his men together and pursues Ishmael and the captives he is taking to Ammon. (Ishmael apparently hopes Ammon will protect him from the inevitable Babylonian reprisals.) Johanan and his troop overtake Ishmael and his captives in Gibeon. The captives are released, though Ishmael escapes with eight men (41:15). Now, Johanan must assume responsibility for the small remainder of Judahites whom he has rescued. They are afraid. He intends to take them to Egypt, because they do not know what the Babylonian army will do when it arrives on the scene. But apparently because of doubts of some of the persons in the group, they stop at Bethlehem to decide whether or not to continue. We are now ready to return to Jeremiah (Jer. 42).

In this narrative of the vicious deeds of Ishmael, Jeremiah plays no active role. The story is a parable in support of the priestly Judean governors of the Persian province of Yehud. The moral is that no one should be so stupid as to attack the only viable form of government. In modern times, we have a proverb that "politics is the art of the possible." That was how the priests and bureaucrats of Yehud understood their own position. The problem is that we cannot know what is possible until alternatives are attempted. Political realism is not false, but it is inherently conservative, and conservatism is not always God's will. It would be false to think of Jeremiah as a conservative, though he must have appeared to many to be so. He genuinely believed it was God's will to submit to the empire of his day, but he never argued that it was a good empire or even that it was the only politically viable alternative. Just that it was God's will, and God's will can hardly be a matter of conservatism. Sometimes it may be fanatical, but that is not because it is conservative but rather because it does not take account of political realities. Thus, the Afghan Talibans believe in obeying God's will, regardless of whether it is Afghan tradition or whether it is politically viable. A political realist like Henry Kissinger could defend the war against Viet Nam, which cost thousands of U.S. and Vietnamese lives, then turn around and negotiate a peace with the Communists, whom he had vilified as inhuman for years. He could do this because he did not operate out of a vision of a good world or obedience to the will of God, but out of an assessment of power relations, how much the U.S. could get out of it, and when it was time to quit because the cost was too high to bear. When doing the will of God, a prophet like Jeremiah is indifferent to "realistic" analysis. In this sense, Jeremiah was closer to the Taliban than to the scribes and officials who drew up the book that bears his name.

Johanan and His Followers Do Not Obey the Word (Jeremiah 42:1—43:7)

The narrative now returns to Jeremiah and the word of God. Gedaliah has been murdered, ending the attempt at provincial home rule under Babylon, and the people who remain have been rescued by Johanan. Now, the text returns to the protagonist, the prophet Jeremiah. We have been told (Jer. 41:17) that Johanan and the people with him intend to go to Egypt to escape imperial control and possible revenge. So, it is a bit surprising to find them consulting Jeremiah in 42:1 about a matter already settled.

Not only do the commanders consult Jeremiah, but they request that he intercede with the Holy One, so that their journey may continue with God's blessing. In verses 3 and 5–6 they go further, swearing that they will do whatever God demands, good or bad (that is, according to their plans or not)—an unexpected piety from military commanders! Jeremiah had been ordered in chapters 11 and 14 not to intercede for this people. His readiness to do so now indicates that with changed circumstances, with Babylon's control now an accomplished fact, the previous order of no intercession is no longer applicable. He promises to make the consultation.

After ten days, an answer comes. No indication is given about how Jeremiah received this answer. The narrator simply presents it as a fact. The answer is in keeping with Jeremiah's message all along. Stay in the land and God will prosper you. Go to Egypt and you will die there and never return to the land. Jeremiah believes that God wills for Judah to submit to Babylon, before, during and after the imperial armies' attack on Jerusalem. To flee to Egypt is to disobey God's word. To stay under Babylonian hegemony in the land is to obey God's word. The remnant believes that by going to Egypt they will escape war and famine but, says Jeremiah, they are wrong; in

Egypt, the Holy One will send sword, famine, and pestilence (Jer. 42:13–17).

Jeremiah apparently knows that Johanan and his forces have already decided on their course of action, for in Jeremiah 42:18–22 he proceeds to detail the deadly outcome of fleeing to Egypt against the word of God. Jeremiah claims that the consultation was a farce all along (and, by implication, that the solemn oath about their willingness to abide by God's answer was a lie).

The answer given by Johanan and Azariah in Jeremiah 43:2 is striking. "You are telling a lie. The Holy One our God did not send you to say, 'Do not go down to Egypt.'" Thus does Jeremiah get a dose of his own medicine. He had many times accused other prophets of prophesying a lie (Jer. 23, 28, and 29). Now it is his turn to receive this accusation. There is no way of adjudicating such accusations, no way of knowing when a prophet is lying or when speaking God's word. The canon legitimates Jeremiah as the true prophet, and so we, who follow the canon as God's revealed word, accept this verdict that in itself is unverifiable. Rather than put all the blame on Jeremiah, Johanan accuses Baruch of being behind Jeremiah's stance. There is no reason to doubt that Baruch shared Jeremiah's pro-Babylonian stance. He was a scribe from one of the great scribal families, and available evidence suggests that these families saw submission as the more viable political alternative for Judah. But neither is there any reason to believe that the scribe did not fully believe that the policy was God's will for Judah.

We should remember that this entire passage is deeply influenced by later political conflict between the Babylonian exile community and that of Egypt. It was the Babylonian exiles who later received the Persian empire's support to reconstruct Jerusalem and Judah. The Bible as we know it is largely the product of scribes from that Babylonian exilic community. In their vision, the Babylonian exile was *the* exile, when *all* Judahites who mattered went into exile and later returned under Cyrus of Persia. They thus divided Israelite "salvation history" into preexilic, exilic, and postexilic periods. This is a truly deceptive division of history, when one takes into account the small numbers of persons actually displaced to Babylon by the empire. The exiles in Babylon did not, of course, consider the exilic community in Egypt to be a legitimate successor to the Judahite state. The section of Jeremiah that we are examining is part of the ideological struggle between those two communities, and it represents the Babylonian exiles' point of view, making no effort to be impartial. The Babylonian exilic community appropriates Jeremiah the prophet for their project, surely in keeping with his own vision of reality, and for this reason they put together the book that today we have in our Bibles.

We should again note that this canonical prophet could accept an empire (Babylon, but not Egypt) as God-given for the punishment of God's people. Empires are not intrinsically evil from the perspective of our Bible. Jeremiah also expects, of course, that God will eventually judge that empire and end its dominion. This is clear from the famous banquet of wrath (Jer. 25:15–29) as well as the poetic oracles against Babylon in Jeremiah 50 and 51. This view was without a doubt that of the historical Jeremiah, as well as the book of Jeremiah. It is more difficult to know whether the support for the Babylonian exiles against the Egyptian ones was also a matter of concern to the historical Jeremiah, but it is most certainly the position of the book of Jeremiah, which is our canonical guide. In spite of his firm convictions, Jeremiah is taken by Johanan to Egypt (Jer. 43:6–7), along with Baruch, obviously against their will though the text is not explicit about this. Thus, to the end, even after he was vindicated by Babylonian control over Judah, Jeremiah found himself in the minority, in opposition. As a prophet, he was never to find social acceptance.

It is difficult to know what all of this might mean to us who are Christians in the twenty-first century. Are we to believe that God wills the church to favor the U.S. empire over its real or potential rivals (the former Soviet Union, China, the European Union, or others)? Or, are we to believe that China or the European Union is God's chosen servant in the twenty-first century? We are not any better equipped for a foolproof adjudication of alternative prophetic visions than was the Egyptian exilic community. The disappearance of the Soviet Union would seem to disqualify it as God's choice in recent times, but there is no way to disqualify the other potential candidates (or to support them). At the least, we must admit that the book of Jeremiah proclaims that submission to a particular empire may well be God's will for a time, and today that empire might be the U.S. empire—a comfortable belief for many Christian churches within the United States but more difficult for Christian churches elsewhere to accept. The difficulty with associating the U.S. empire with God's will for the world is that it is, for U.S. Christian churches, the easy, socially acceptable, even patriotic, position—hardly what Jeremiah leads us to expect for those who embrace God's will.

Symbolic Babylonian Control over Egypt (Jeremiah 43:8–13)

This short unit describes a symbolic action that God enjoins on Jeremiah. He is to bury some large stones under the door to Pharaoh's house in Tahpanhes. These stones, he is to explain, represent the foundation for the throne that the king of Babylon will erect to govern over Egypt. Thus, the flight to Egypt is futile. Even Egypt, the second major power in the world of those days, is to come under the control of Babylon, for Nebuchadrezzar (as Nebuchadnezzar is called here) is "my servant" (43:10), an expression added in MT to underline the theological significance of the geopolitical arrangements of the time.

Jeremiah Debates with the Egyptian Exiles (Jeremiah 44:1–30)

The narrative about the fall of Jerusalem ended in chapter 43. Chapter 44 presents discourse of the Deuteronomy-like style that Mowinckel called the C-corpus (see pp. 00). As we would expect, Jeremiah has the principal speeches (44:1–14, 20–23, and 24–30). These speeches repeat well-worn themes that have appeared on many previous occasions in the book. What makes this chapter interesting is the speech with which the exiles try to refute Jeremiah (44:15–19). But let us take things in order.

In his first speech (Jer. 44:1–14), said to be pronounced in Egypt, Jeremiah reminds his listeners of the Holy One's efforts to turn the people from their evil ways. God has repeatedly sent the prophets to call Israel to repentance, but it has been in vain. Judah and Jerusalem have persisted in their evil ways. The refugees in Egypt have continued the evil ways of their ancestors, and so the Holy One will bring upon them the sword, famine, and pestilence, and they shall never return to the land for which they long.

The response of the people is surprising for its boldness. The spokesmen and their wives declare in a most forthright fashion that they will not listen to (that is, obey) the word that Jeremiah pronounces. Instead, they will continue sacrificing to the Queen of Heaven and fulfilling the vows they have vowed to her. In fact, they offer an alternative theological interpretation of the disasters that have befallen Judah and Jerusalem. While offerings were made to the Queen of Heaven in Jerusalem, there was abundance and they knew no misfortune (44:17). It was when these offerings were abandoned that the troubles began. So now, they will faithfully fulfill their obligations to the Queen of Heaven and not respond to Jeremiah's calls to return to fidelity to the Holy One, who took them out of bondage in the house of Egypt.

The cessation of sacrifices to the Queen of Heaven would have come as part of Josiah's reform, when all cults other than that of the Holy One were abolished by royal decree. This, say the exiles, was the beginning of the troubles that culminated in Nebuchadnezzar's invasion of Judah and destruction of Jerusalem and its temple. A bold ploy indeed! Such an argument cannot be refuted. It is a matter of historical interpretation, and in such interpretations several posibilities are equally available. The argument of the exiles is, indeed, very powerful, and there is no way in which Jeremiah can refute it, since he too abides by the premise that historical disasters are the result of having displeased one's god or gods. He is reduced in his final speeches to repeating the "official" explanation, that the reform was insufficient. This argument cannot be resolved rationally. Jeremiah has the advantage of representing the dominant line of theology in the Bible, but that advantage is not a rational argument. For a determined minority, it will carry little weight.

One is reminded of the arguments between economists today about the origin and solution to the massive problem of poverty in today's globalized economy. The "official" line is that the problems result from too much government and labor union interference with the rule of the market, and the "solution" is more market. The minority view says that it is precisely the domination of the market that has caused poverty on this scale, and the solution is to regulate the market and encourage unions so that the market produces what people need and salaries are adequate for living. Like Jeremiah's argument with the exiles, this argument can never be resolved rationally. It is a matter of interpretation, and excellent cases can be made on both sides. The "more market" view has the advantage today because it is in control of the global economy, but its arguments are insufficient to carry the day in academic debate. This is all much like the situation that Jeremiah faced in Egypt with the Judahite exiles who insisted on their alternative theological interpretation of the end of the kingdom of Judah.

One last comment: In the context of the book of Jeremiah, where the dominant perspective is that promoted by the Babylonian exilic community, the speech by the Egyptian exiles serves to discredit them as spokespersons for an illegitimate and lost cause, that of an Israelite people without an exclusive loyalty to the Holy One who rescued them from bondage in Egypt. This is the canonical view, and even though one may sympathize with the alternative argument, one must in the end admit that it lost out. The community of the Egyptian exile lost out to the community of the Babylonian exile. History cannot be redone in reverse. Persuasive as the case might be, there is no reversing the verdict of history after all these centuries. Will this also be the historical verdict on the "more market" view? Maybe, but perhaps not. With such massive global poverty apparently increasing at an uncontainable rate, the jury of history is still out.

An Oracle for Baruch (Jeremiah 45:1–5)

This section ends with a private oracle addressed to Baruch, the scribe who wrote the book in Jeremiah 36 and who was accused of inciting Jeremiah in Jeremiah 43. Like the earlier message to Ebed-Melech, the functionary who saved Jeremiah's life (Jer. 39:15–18), this is a private oracle, and the two show many similarities. Both begin by repeating the general threat against the people and offer to the persons addressed a minor recompense, their lives as booty in the midst of the calamity.

The oracle for Baruch begins with a quotation of the scribe's words (Jer. 45:2) that shows him to be discouraged. To be Jeremiah's scribe is an unpopular task, since the scribe is detested along with the prophet by their people. This oracle comes fairly early in Jeremiah's ministry, the fourth year of Jehoiakim, the year of the incident with the scroll (chap. 36). In the LXX text of Jeremiah, this oracle for Baruch comes right before the closing chapter, which summarizes the exile (Jer. 52). In the canonical Jeremiah (MT), in which the oracles against the nations have been displaced to the end (chaps. 46—51), the Baruch oracle wraps up the account of the collapse of Jerusalem. Chronologically, this is not its place, but we have seen many times that the order of MT Jeremiah is governed by thematic rather than chronological concerns.

In Jeremiah 45:5, the Holy One states of Baruch that he seeks great things for himself. This, says God, is out of place. His is a time of uprooting and tearing down, not of planting and building up. Grandiose dreams are out of place in such times. But God does make the same offer made on various occasions to others. If he will obey God's word, Baruch will have his life as a booty of battle. A modest prize, but something nevertheless. The general structure of this oracle reminds the reader of Jeremiah 12:1–5, where Jeremiah's complaint is answered in a similar fashion.

The book of Jeremiah is not interested in Baruch as a person but only as the instrument of Jeremiah. His is a minor part in the historical drama of the collapse of the nation, but an honorable one considering his fidelity to the word of God. The implication is that there are times when true believers must be ready to accept small parts and small prizes in the midst of terrible times. Fortunately, this is not yet the case in our globalized world, but the calamitous growth of poverty augurs the proximity of such times. To the last generation, Jeremiah was still offering some hope if they would submit to Babylon. Perhaps we, too, can find similar hope for our world, if we repent of our ways and make a priority of combatting the cancer of poverty that is engulfing our world! May God help us!

PART B'

Prophecies to the Nations
(Jeremiah 46—51)

The six long chapters that deal with the surrounding nations are an important component in the structure of the book of Jeremiah. These chapters draw the preaching of Jeremiah to a close, underlined in the words of Jeremiah 51:64, "Thus far are the words of Jeremiah." Most of Jeremiah's preaching and actions in the previous chapters have been addressed to Judah and the dwellers of Jerusalem, even though Jeremiah has been appointed a prophet to the nations (Jer. 1:5) and God has said to him, "Today I appoint you over nations and over kingdoms, to pluck up and to pull down, to destroy and to overthrow, to build and to plant" (Jer. 1:10). Of course, the nations play a prominent role in the very center of the book, in the poem about the banquet in which God will make them drink the cup of God's wrath (Jer. 25:15–29). Now, in these final poems, Jeremiah directly addresses the nations one by one to perform the task for which he was appointed in the beginning.

In the overall ring structure, chapters 46—51 balance Jeremiah 1:4–19. The reader, moving linearly, begins with the global vision of the mission of this prophet, only to "forget" it as she reads the threats to Judah. Those threats do, of course, come in the shape of an invasion by an unnamed enemy from the north. Beginning with 20:4, the enemy is named as Babylon, which appears at the gates of Jerusalem in 21:1–10 and is from then on a constant presence, although not addressed directly. The tension builds up until the banquet scene in Jeremiah 25:15–29, after which it relaxes a bit, especially with the interlude of the chapters of hope in 30—33. Chapters 39—45 recount the depressing final days of Judah and Jerusalem, facing trouble not only from Babylon but also from internal struggles that lead to the assassination of the governor Gedaliah. Finally, with these six chapters addressed to the nations, the reader feels that the wording of the prophet's call in Jeremiah 1 is justified.

The ring structure of the book is far from obvious, and the reader who runs through the book in the normal way will not detect it. A comparison with the penultimate version of the book, which we have in the LXX, proves that the book was not written in the ring format. Rather, the parts were rearranged to give the whole a structure that focuses on Babylon, because that is where the exile community, the community of the editors in the Persian province of Yehud, had spent two generations. This gives the book as we have it its shape.

Most of the poems in chapters 46—51 are addressed, at least poetically, to the kings and/or peoples of one or another nation in the area surrounding Judah. Nevertheless, at several points in these poems we find sections addressed to Judah. In fact, it is difficult to imagine how a prophet from a small and poor country like Judah could effectively address the king or the people of even a nearby nation like Ammon, much less a distant and powerful nation like Babylon. We do have a short passage, Jeremiah 51:59–64, in which the scribe Seraiah is instructed to read a book written by Jeremiah in Babylon, although where in Babylon and to whom is unclear. The operative part of this action is what follows. Seraiah is to tie a stone to the book (scroll, of course) and throw it into the river, where it will sink and never rise again. The words of Jeremiah announce the fall of the Babylonian empire, and the action of Seraiah is to act out the contents of a book whose reading would have no effect on a rich and arrogant people like the Babylonians.

This sort of action, a symbolic curse on the enemies, is what people expected from their prophets—and Judahites got precious little of what they expected from Jeremiah! These instructions to Seraiah, which were presumably carried out as requested, and the whole collection of poems concerning the nations are addressed to the nations for the benefit of the Judean people and their rulers. Judah and Jerusalem are to "overhear" the words to Edom, Egypt, and the rest, and the poems were really written for Judah and Jerusalem, though imaginatively addressed to other peoples. The Judeans must know that their God, the Holy One who rescued them from Egyptian bondage, rules the nations of the world. It is the Holy One who has turned them and the rest of the nations of the world over to Babylonian domination, so that the king of Babylon is really the servant of the Holy One, carrying out a plan of which the king has no knowledge. Judah's people need to know that the Holy One will visit Babylon with destruction and bring back the people of Israel from the many nations in which they have been dispersed.

So, the oracles concerning the nations are really intended to be heard by the people of Judah and their rulers, rather than by the peoples to whom they are ostensibly addressed. Although this "prophet to the nations" has a sphere of action confined to a small, peripheral nation in what we today call the ancient Near East, he gives his people a global perspective that offers hope in the end.

In the LXX, this collection of oracles follows the words against Zedekiah during the siege of Jerusalem in Jeremiah 25:1–13. The collection ends with the banquet scene, which is 25:15–29 in MT Jeremiah but 32:15–29 in LXX Jeremiah. Thus, in LXX these oracles are the middle of the book. According to the hypothesis that LXX reflects an older Hebrew version of Jeremiah and MT a later revision of that Hebrew original (see the Introduction, pp. 4–5), one can assert that the oracles against the nations were relocated to the end of the book to provide a fitting climax to the poems and narratives of the "prophet to the nations." Although the rearrangement was drastic, the final improvement is clear, at least to this reader.

The internal arrangement of the poems in Jeremiah 46—51 is very significant, beginning as they do with poems concerning Egypt and ending as they do with poems concerning Babylon (this poem about Babylon is by far the longest section of the poems against the nations). According to Jeremiah's preaching, all the other nations have been given to Babylon as punishment for their evils. Since chapter 21, Jeremiah has been calling for Judah and Jerusalem and the other nations to submit to Babylon, because that is the plan and the will of the Holy One. Among the nations, Babylon is a special case. To Babylon, Jeremiah devotes two long chapters (Jer. 50—51). Here, finally, it becomes clear that Babylon will be punished for swallowing the other nations, even when this was the plan of the Holy One. So, to end this book with Babylon is a major turn within the whole. Let us now proceed to read these oracles concerning nations that no longer exist but which were important to Judah in the days of Jeremiah and also in the days of Yehud's reconstruction under Persia.

Egypt (Jeremiah 46:1–28)

The oracles concerning the nations begin with a general introduction in Jeremiah 46:1, which is not in the LXX. (It is, therefore, part of the

MT's editorial ordering.) The rest of chapter 46 is devoted to Egypt, containing at least two oracles against Egypt (Jer. 46:3–12 and 46:14–24), a brief prose portion both negative and positive concerning Egypt (46:25–26), and an oracle of salvation for Israel (46:27–28).

The chapter concerning Egypt is well organized. It begins with a call to an unnamed army to prepare for battle by donning weapons and accessories of war (Jer. 46:3–4). Verses 5–6 shift to the perspective of an unnamed observer who describes the route of the Egyptian warriors because of an enemy from the north in the region of the Euphrates. The warriors all flee and none turns around to make a stand. Verses 7–9 describe the might of the Egyptian army, strengthened by soldiers from Cush, Put, and Lydia. They fully expect to sweep over the earth and leave the cities without dwellers.

The next strophe, Jeremiah 46:10–16, identifies the real enemy of Egypt: Lord YHWH of the hosts. Since the word conventionally translated "hosts" really means armies, this expression refers to the Holy One in militaristic mode. It is God's day of vengeance on enemies. The Holy One has called for a feast in the land of the north by the Euphrates, at which the sword will drink its fill of blood.

Here we reach the heart of not just this oracle but all the oracles concerning the nations. The battles that take place on the Euphrates or anywhere else are really part of the plans of God. The real agent of Egypt's downfall is the Holy One of Israel. It is not really necessary to know which nation and which army will bring about the Holy One's vengeance on Egypt. Geopolitical analyses, though helpful, do not get at the heart of what moves history.

This is, obviously, a theological understanding of history, which takes its starting point in faith. As far as Egypt and its leaders are concerned, the military incursion to the Euphrates has little or nothing to do with Israel, and they have no reason to take into account the God of a nation that is for them just a convenient bridge to the Mesopotamian region. But from the perspective of the prophet who created this poem, everything hinges on the purposes of the Holy One of Israel. The power of the poetry is not its capacity to move the Egyptians but its ability to give Israelites a true perspective on world events.

The editorial comment in Jeremiah 46:13 mentions a Babylonian invasion of Egypt led by King Nebuchadnezzar, here called Nebuchadrezzar (v. 13 follows up on the editorial comment in 46:2 that linked the first oracle to the Egyptian incursion into the upper Euphrates at Carchemish). The second oracle then opens with a call to unnamed persons to announce the work of the sword to various cities of Egypt. Egypt was a powerful nation, aspiring to be the empire of the day. But, says Jeremiah, Egypt's bull has fled because the Holy One has pushed it (46:15).

Egypt's "bull" represents its royal ideology, centered on the divine bull Apis. Any empire or aspiring empire needs an ideology, a global world-picture within which to justify its pretensions. In recent history, we might think of Soviet pretensions to challenge the hegemony of its allies in the Great War against fascism (which we call World War II). No one can doubt that the defeat of German plans to establish a Third Reich was wrought in the icy plains of Russia by the Red Army, but that army failed to rise from its enormous casualties to claim its role as a first-rate world power. Like Egypt in the seventh and sixth centuries B.C.E., proclaiming its god Apis as a benefactor who produced the fertilizing floods of the Nile, so the USSR claimed to be the avant-garde of a universal condition of justice for all humankind, Communism. In the name of this god, nations and even communists who "stood in the way of the progress of history" could be sacrificed. It was a powerful worldview capable of challenging even the Free Democratic Market god of the United States.

However, any imperial ideology is idolatry for Jeremiah. From the prophet's perspective, the outcome of imperial conflicts is not due to religion or worldview but to the God of Israel, who created heaven and earth. In geopolitical terms, we might say that the Egyptian military apparatus was no match for that of Babylon, nor the Soviet one for that of the United States and its Western European allies. But our text insists that military analyses do not settle the outcome of conflicts. They are settled by the Holy One of Israel, who champions widows, orphans, and strangers (Deut. 10:16–19). The first strophe of this second oracle, Jeremiah 46:14–16, names the reality factor of the Holy One (46:15) and the collapse of the Egyptians before the destroying sword (46:16).

The next strophe, Jeremiah 46:17–19, invites an unnamed people to call the Pharaoh a braggart. The real king is not he but the Holy One of Israel (46:18), who stands out like Carmel into the sea. (Carmel is a mountain mass that juts into the Mediterranean Sea near modern Haifa.) In verse 19, the Holy One calls to the Egyptians to pack their bags for exile. The most striking images in the next strophe are the horsefly from the north that "bugs" the beautiful heifer of Egypt (46:20) and the woodsmen who cut down her forests (46:22–23). The final editorial comment in Jeremiah 46:25–26, mostly missing in LXX, reinforces what was already expressed in the poetry: All in Egypt, including its gods, are victims of what is happening. But then, surprisingly, a brief prose statement (added in MT) adds that afterwards Egypt shall be inhabited as before—a truly surprising statement from Israel and Israel's God to a nation that, after Babylon, is the archetypal symbol of the enemy!

The final poem, an oracle of promise and salvation addressed to Jacob/ Israel, requires no comment. If the God of Israel determines world history, the people of Israel play a very special role in that history. From the point of view of faith, this applies for Christians today as also to other people of faith in our times, among whom we should include at least Jews and Muslims and probably other peoples of faith as well.

The Philistines (Jeremiah 47:1–7)

The image of raging waters and the roar of oncoming armies dominate this well-wrought little poem against the Philistines, which ends with a reflection on the "sword of the Holy One." The editorial work of the last edition is quite evident and seems well done. The introduction in MT specifies that the Philistines are the intended object. (The LXX makes this a general poem against "foreigners," which covers Tyre and Sidon in Jer. 47:4 along with the Philistines of 47:4, 5, and 7). The MT also adds mention of their origin in Caphtor (Crete). The Philistines resided in the coastal plain of Judah, an area that had military significance as the best passageway for an army heading from or to Egypt. The Philistines were no threat to Judah in Jeremiah's time, though the texts of the books of Samuel kept alive an historic rivalry. The point of this and other oracles concerning the minor kingdoms surrounding Judah has less to do with specifics of international relations than with establishing that the Holy One is in control of history and intends to turn all kingdoms over to Nebuchadnezzar, king of Babylon.

The "waters from the north" that open this poem are not literal or physical waters, for there is no source of water north of the Philistine cities. It is probably an allusion to the Euphrates, an allusion that calls to mind Isa. 8:5–8. In any case, this raging flood from the north will sweep away cities and their dwellers. The frightening sound of horses' hooves and heavy military wagons (Jer. 47:3) will cause parents to abandon their children in headlong flight, a dramatic idea because it seems unlikely in a real calamity. In Jeremiah 47:4, the cause of this flood from the north is identified, and it is no surprise to the reader of Jeremiah that it is the Holy One. This fine poem ends with an appeal to God's sword to return to its scabbard. The appeal is useless, because God has appointed the sword to this task. This may be a reflection on Babylon, or our current empire, as the instrument of God, which can hardly cease to perform the tasks for which God has sent it. But such instrumental status did not mean to Jeremiah, nor does it mean today, that empires are immune to divine judgment. That part comes a bit later in our book.

Concerning Moab (Jeremiah 48:1–47)

There is a surprisingly large collection of oracles concerning Moab in this chapter. The kingdom of Moab was Judah's neighbor across the Jordan River to the east. Moab was, according to the stories in Genesis, a descendant of Lot, Abraham's nephew. A close relationship was thus felt with this neighbor. The stories of the desert under the leadership of Moses give a lot of consideration to Moab, and Moses' final speech, now found in the book of Deuteronomy, was pronounced on the plains of Moab across the river from Jericho. Much of Moabite territory, what lay north of the Arnon river, was assigned to Gad in the distribution described in the book of Joshua (a narrative reflecting dispute over territorial limits). The Moabite king Mesha quarreled with Israel over this land in the ninth century B.C.E., a dispute reflected in the biblical books of Kings and in the Moabite Stone uncovered by archaeologists.

The tone of Jeremiah's Moabite poems is set by the first one, Jeremiah 48:1–6, which has the form of a lament or dirge such as would be sung over a corpse at a funeral. The lament names several cities of Moab, many of which are impossible for modern scholars to locate, and cries *hoy* ("woe") over them. The reason for this death of a nation and its cities is a "sword" (48:2). In the context of the book of Jeremiah, it is clear that the Holy One has turned all nations over to the sword of Babylon, and in Jeremiah 27 the prophet urges all the kings to surrender without resistance. So, the reader of Jeremiah 48 may assume that verse 2 refers to God's sword, which was at that time the king of Babylon. The second section of this poem (48:3–5) calls attention to the cries of the people of Moab, especially their little ones. The anguish is general. The poem ends with a dramatic call for the people to flee from their land in order to save their lives. It is a neat little funeral dirge.

The following poem, Jeremiah 48:7–8, gets at the cause of this sad situation. The small nation of Moab has placed its trust in its works and treasures! But neither works of civilization nor buildings nor treasures are a sufficient protection from the designs of Israel's Holy One. As a result, Moab's national god, Chemosh, will be taken into exile along with his priests and princes. Every city and region of Moab will be utterly destroyed. When nations trust in their great works and in their abundant treasures, they perish, as Moab will surely perish according to this poem.

In a continuation of what almost seems like a catalogue of the false hopes of this nation, the poem contained in Jeremiah 48:14–17 calls attention to Moab's armies. In any nation, even a small one, there may be pride in the military forces, their modern equipment, and their brave spirit. But it is no use. The choicest youths of Moab are heading for slaughter.

Calamity is near, and the word of God makes its arrival inescapable. The neighbors will soon marvel at how Moab's glorious forces have been cut off.

Probably the finest poetry of this chapter comes in Jeremiah 48:40–44. The poem opens by announcing that "he" (perhaps Babylon) will swoop down like an eagle on Moab and attack. Towns and fortifications will fall. Moab's mighty warriors will cry out like a woman in labor (but will have nothing to show for their pain). Their problem is that they "made themselves great" before the Holy One (48:42). A nation cannot survive if it ignores the reality of God. Verses 43 and 44 play on the similar sounds of terror (*pahad*), pit (*pahat*), and trap (*pah*), creating an effect difficult to capture in translation. Poetry is not simply a set of meanings but also the play of rhythm, alliteration, and cadence. In this case, the insistent drumming of the p-consonants with the a-vowels communicates the entrapment of which the translation speaks. There is no escaping the enclosing circle of judgment on Moab, its cities, and their mighty and small inhabitants.

The tone for this collection of prose and poetic pieces is set by the dirge that began with its lament of *hoy* in 48:1. This is wrapped up with the *'oy* in 48:46. But then comes a surprise: Verse 47 announces the Holy One's plan to restore Moab's fortunes (*shavti shevuth-mo'av*) in the latter days. This is a surprising announcement, coming as it does from a prophet in Moab's small rival across the Jordan River, Judah! It looks like an addition, a judgment confirmed by its absence in LXX. But such an important addition! The God of Israel is also the God of Moab. Just as Jerusalem's destruction cannot be the end for Judah, neither can the destruction of Heshbon and Horonaim be the end of Moab. This is a lesson in the governance of God the Creator over all nations.

Concerning Ammon (Jeremiah 49:1–6)

Ammon was another of Israel's transjordanian neighbors, one that played a much smaller role in her history than that of Moab. The Ammonites were thought to be descended, like the Moabites, from Abraham's nephew Lot (Gen. 19:38), and they were, hence, perceived as related. The saying concerning Ammon comes after that about Moab and before that about Edom; these three were close neighbors, although the geographical sequence from south to north would have been Edom, Moab, Ammon.

The first part of this poem, Jeremiah 49:1–2, deals with a dispute over land between Israel and Ammon. Words from the "inherit" family appear four times in these two verses. "Children has Israel none? An *heir* is there none? Why does Milcom [Ammon's patron god] *disinherit* Gad and his people settle in its towns? Therefore, surely days are coming, says the Holy One, when I will make to be heard in Rabbath Ammon [Ammon's capital] the war cry, and it shall become a desolate mound and its high places burnt with fire, so Israel shall *possess* her *dispossessors*, says the Holy One." The problem is a familiar one, a territorial dispute between two peoples who have claims on the same land. The oracle is framed as a legal indictment and its subsequent verdict, from the perspective of Israel. God is the accuser and God the one who executes the sentence of war against Ammon. Set within the book of Jeremiah as the oracle is, the reader must presume that the instrument of war is Babylon, even though in this case the cause of war is an injustice to Israel and the result is legal restitution for Israel.

The second part of this oracle, Jeremiah 49:3–5, reverts to the form we have come to expect from Jeremiah's oracles concerning the nations. As with Moab and its god Chemosh (Jer. 48:7), Ammon and its god Milcom will go into exile, along with the god's priests and princes. In fact, verse 7b against Moab and verse 3b against Ammon are almost identical in language. Also like the accusation against Moab is that against the daughter of Ammon for trusting in her treasures (49:4). She is confident that any enemy can be bought off: "Who will come against me?" But the Holy One in person will disperse the Ammonites so that nobody will be able to gather them (49:5).

The oracle against Ammon is a piece well done, although, coming as it does after Moab, it lacks originality. The final verse (49:6) promises restoration after exile and dispersion, in tension with the preceding verse's statement that nobody will be able to gather the dispersed Ammonites. This verse, like the promise to Moab in Jeremiah 48:47, was added by the MT's editors. It is significant that the final word even on Israel's rivals is, in these cases, one of hope. Even when judgment is pronounced because of wrongs to God's people, God's will for the evildoers is their return to live in peace in their lands, perhaps even the lands disputed by Ammon and Gad-Israel. This ending gives us some reason to call for a negotiated settlement to territorial disputes like the one that wracks Israel and Palestine in our time. Today, we have an arbiter in the form of the United Nations, something that Jeremiah had to leave to God. This gives us some real possibility of getting some distance from the law of the strongest that tends to prevail in international politics. It is important for God's people today to support the solutions that organizations such as the United Nations can propose. Otherwise, hope for humanity must seem dim and we would have to remain with the damning condemnations of LXX Jeremiah, which offers no hope for Moab or for Ammon.

Concerning Edom (Jeremiah 49:7–22)

Edom was a neighbor to Judah on the south and southeast. It was known for two things, its dwellings in the rocky crags, including cities carved out of the sandstone, and its wisdom. Historically, its relations with Judah were not good. A small book of the Bible, Obadiah, is an oracle directed against Edom with considerable venom for Edom's treatment of Judahite refugees at the time of Judah's collapse. Portions of Jeremiah 49:7–22 coincide with poetic lines in Obadiah, but it is not clear which book has influenced the other. Furthermore, not all the books of the Hebrew Bible share this dim view of the Edomites. In Deuteronomy 23, Ammonites and Moabites are excluded from the assembly of Israel, but Edomites, presumably the grandchildren of Edomite immigrants, are permitted to enter in the third generation.

Most of the Edom section is taken up by a poem that runs from Jeremiah 49:7 to 49:16. Verses 12–13 are a prose interruption. The style shows a lot of wisdom influence, appropriate for an oracle about a nation reputed for its wisdom. In good wisdom style, the poem begins with questions about Edom's wisdom (49:7). Commands to flee the "calamity of Esau" that "I" (God) am bringing on him suggest that Edomite wisdom will be proven if indeed its dwellers flee the catastrophe. Fleeing is a violent disruption of any family's life, yet in times of imminent danger it may be the only route to survival. When the Nazis came to power in 1933, some Jewish families fled to Switzerland, England, or other countries fearing for their lives. But Germany's Jewish families were also German, many having lived in Germany for many generations and being well established as participants in German society, and most Jews resisted the trauma of emigration—with disastrous results. In retrospect, one can judge that those who fled in the early months of the Nazi government showed exceptional wisdom and were rewarded with their lives for their wisdom. The prophet sees the people of Edom faced with a similar challenge that will prove whether their reputation for wisdom is deserved or not. It is God who brings "Esau's calamity." It will be total. The images of the vineyard workers who always leave some grapes behind on the vine or the thief at night who takes only what he can sell or use are a powerful way of expressing the disaster from which Edom must flee. Verse 11, surprisingly, affirms the Holy One's protection for the orphans and widows who will be left. The only reason given in this poem for the coming calamity is Edom's pride, reflected in its dwelling in the heights of the mountains among the clefts in the rocks (49:16). But rock fortresses will be of no use on the day of God's "visitation."

We live in a time of mass violence when fleeing may well be the best way to save one's life and one's family. One thinks of Viet Nam or Afghanistan, threatened with total devastation by our current empire. It is terrible to be uprooted from the land one knows and loves, but survival is often worth that awful loss. Support for refugees is in our time a very high human and Christian virtue. Countries like Pakistan and Iran, which have received enormous waves of refugees, merit international support.

Concerning Damascus (Jeremiah 49:23–27)

Damascus was a beautiful city in a well-watered location at the foot of mountains surrounded by dry desert. Still, it is surprising to hear it referred to in this poem (Jer. 49:25) as "my delight," presumably God's. Jeremiah's oracle concerning Damascus, which also includes the Syrian cities of Hamath and Arpad (49:23), is a cry of anguish at the destruction there. Without further qualification that destruction is God's responsibility ("I will kindle a fire," 49:27) with no mention of a human agent. Nor is any cause for the divine action offered. The poem underscores the contrast between the delights "before" and the anguish "after." There is no escaping God's action in history. Syria was an intermediate power, like Korea, Brazil, or South Africa in our days. It, like the small kingdoms of Ammon, Moab, or Edom, must submit to God's plans for the universe.

Concerning Kedar (Jeremiah 49:28–33)

This oracle concerns the bedouin peoples of the Arabian desert, beyond the kingdoms of Edom, Moab, and Ammon. They were herders, and camels were their principal animal. What strikes the prophet as remarkable is that they have no doors or bars and count for their protection on their isolation (Jer. 49:31). As is often the case in the oracles concerning the nations, these people are urged to flee for their lives (49:30). The Hazor mentioned in the introduction and in verses 30 and 33 is a mystery; it must be a region, since a permanent settlement would not suit the lifestyle of these wandering desert people. The MT text mentions Nebuchadrezzar (again, alternative for Nebchadnezzar) in 49:30, as well as in the heading of the prophecy (49:28). Though this king is said to "have a plan" against Kedar, the reader of Jeremiah knows that the ultimate plans in human history are those of God. The king of Babylon (so LXX in verse 30) is no more than God's instrument.

In looking back on the way we have come in our reading of these oracles, we see that the might of the Egyptians, the wealth of the Ammonites, the high crags of the Edomites, and the isolation of Kedar are all equally useless as protection when the plan of God is to destroy kingdoms and turn them over to the empire of the day.

Concerning Elam (Jeremiah 49:34–39)

Elam is the farthest from Judah of any of the nations in this collection. It was east of Mesopotamia. Elam was a very ancient nation located in the region of Susiana controlled by the ancient city of Susa. It had its own language that was unrelated to either Mesopotamian or Iranian languages, and its history as a distinct nation goes back to around 3200 B.C.E. Susa became one of the capitals of Cyrus of Persia in the period when the book of Jeremiah was being prepared, but its origins were not Persian. Its history is closely tied to that of the Mesopotamian cities to its west. It is not obvious why the book of Jeremiah should devote a section to Elam. Perhaps Elamite participation in the Persian empire is the justification, though the editors of Jeremiah were not anti-Persian. This is a very severe oracle. Every line begins with the first person singular of divinity, "I will…," followed by action verbs of destruction and dispersion. It is, then, a poem of few images but pounding, driving singleness of purpose. The Holy One is the sole agent of this ruin, in a fashion that is inescapable, even brutal in its directness.

It is all the more striking, then, that the last word is a promise of restoration (Jer. 49:39), as we have found in the oracles concerning Egypt, Moab, and Ammon. All of these promises are absent from the LXX Jeremiah and are, hence, editorial additions in the later MT revision of the book. They are important, and we must take them seriously. Enemies are for the time being. In the end, we are all sons and daughters of the same God!

Against Babylon (Jeremiah 50:1—51:58)

The collection of oracles against Babylon is far and away the largest of the sayings against nations. The very size of this collection shows the special nature of Babylon among the nations. This is *the* empire; it cannot be treated like just another nation.

In a sense, the whole book of Jeremiah is a prophecy concerning Babylon. The enemy from the north dominates chapters 2—19. Beginning with chapter 20, that enemy gets a name, Babylon. Subsequent chapters continue to describe Babylon's advance against Judah and the nations, a march that appears inexorable. Babylon's power is out of proportion to the defensive capacities of the other nations. There is no mediating League of Nations or United Nations—just Babylon and then all the rest. Of course, in any century of human history, empires dream of claiming the world as a stage to demonstrate their might. Each nation must recognize Babylon's hegemony. Some, like Egypt or Elam, can negotiate the terms of their dependence and appear as allies. Egypt was a wealthy country with an incredibly rich production of grain, and it was far enough from Babylon to make military expeditions costly and undesirable for that empire. Elam was strategically located just east of Mesopotamia, in the rise to the Iranian plateau that was the launching area for trade with the producers of the eastern nations of what we call Asia today. But most nations were small and helpless, totally at the mercy of Babylon. Such was Judah, along with Edom,

Moab, Ammon, and even Syria. Even here there was room for minor maneuvers. One might readily submit, avoiding a destructive invasion and hoping for favored nation status in the Babylonian world order. Or one might, like Judah, be a troublemaker, allying with other minor states to resist in the hope of gaining concessions. This was a dangerous policy, but it offered the satisfaction of a certain amount of national dignity within an unfair world order.

Throughout his ministry, Jeremiah spoke a single message. Judah must not play troublemaker but must submit willingly to the Babylonian king. Only thus would Judah gain its survival as spoils of battle and not face total destruction. This seems like a very practical, realistic, assessment of the power relations in his world. It is, to draw a contemporary analogy, to recommend the road of Costa Rica and not that of Cuba in a world dominated by the U.S. empire. There may be no glory in being a submissive client, but one does at least survive and sometimes retain some minor cultural autonomy in a world shaped by U.S. singers, movies, and news agencies. Or, in a contemporary parallel to the Davidic kings of Judah, a small nation might choose the Cuban path. Such a nation risks annihilation by a vastly superior military force but takes seriously the United Nations' call for a world in which all nations have a voice in common decisions (even if, inevitably, the wealthy nations have a louder voice than the smaller ones, via their permanent seats in the Security Council). In exchange for the sacrifices of being an outsider in a U.S.-dominated world, such a nation can maintain its national culture, some measure of national economic control, and, more importantly, keep alive alternatives for the day when the U.S. empire collapses, so that the world is not left with a void, needing to start again from scratch. In our world, countries like China and India play this important historic role, but Cuba, a very small nation, is joining them as a "nonaligned" nation in the former bipolar world and an "outsider" nation in today's monopolar world. But Cuba's people pay a high cost in daily sacrifices to live as outsiders in a world economy dominated by the U.S. empire. In Judah, the kings pushed a "Cuban" model while Jeremiah advocated a "Costa Rican" model of submission to empire. All of the book of Jeremiah is dominated by this conflict of models.

But Jeremiah was a prophet and not a political analyst. For him, submission to Babylon was the plan and the will of God, as is especially clear in his mission to the ambassadors of the small nations gathered in Jerusalem, reported in Jeremiah 27. The Creator orders all nations, peoples, and beasts to submit to "Nebuchadnezzar, my servant." Jeremiah as an inspired prophet (and his successors who edited the book) had no doubt that this was the genuine will of God, disagreement with which was tantamount to rebellion against the Creator of the universe. Throughout the reigns of Jehoiakim and Zedekiah, the prophet had single-mindedly, in many settings and diverse manners, preached this submission to Babylon. This single-mindedness makes the oracles against Babylon a very significant climax to Jeremiah's preaching. He says with all his poetic resources that Babylon's hour has finally come, and God will pay her for her arrogant deeds against God's people and the other nations of the world! Jeremiah is no Francis Fukuyama, the U.S. State Department advisor who interprets the Global Market in an astoundingly arrogant fashion as the "end of history." Fukuyama says that no more significant changes can occur, for a stable and enduring system has been achieved against which it is folly and culpable sin to rebel. For Jeremiah, by contrast, Babylon is God's *provisional* instrument to right the wrongs of the world, but when its task is fulfilled, its day of judgment will arrive. And that is the content of this final blast in Jeremiah chapters 50 and 51!

Talk about God's plan for history does raise some theological problems for us. Jeremiah and Isaiah often refer to a divine plan, to which they are privy. If we believe that God makes a difference in history, that God should have plans for history is a natural conclusion—but a problematic one. Any nation at war (excepting the Soviet Union with its official atheistic stance), believes itself to be an instrument of God, whether for democracy, against drug trafficking or terrorism, for civilizing the world, or Christianizing or Islamicizing it. How are we to weigh such claims? Says the writer of Ecclesiastes, "Never be rash with your mouth, nor let your heart be quick to utter a word before God, for God is in heaven, and you upon earth; therefore let your words be few" (Eccl. 5:2, NRSV). We must speak of God's works and God's plans, but we must never forget that we do not know finally what they are. Jeremiah was impossibly confident that he knew the unknowable. We accept his specific historical judgments because the canonization process has consecrated them. But had we been present for the debate between Jeremiah and Hananiah (Jer. 29), we could not have rendered a conclusive word about which prophet spoke the word of God, only our opinion based on what would lead to better human living conditions.

Babylon will be totally wasted (Jeremiah 50:2–10). This poem begins with an unnamed speaker addressing imperatives to "you" (second person plural, Jer. 50:2). There follow several lines (50:3–7) about "them" (third person plural), presumably by the same speaker, who is revealed by the reference to "my people" in verse 6 as the Holy One. The poem ends with several lines of imperatives addressed to Israel/Judah (50:8–10).

Verse 2 calls for proclamation of the coming destruction of Babylon and its gods. Placed in a collection of prophecies of Jeremiah, who lived and died under Babylonian rule, this is a very bold statement. It seems out of line with the prophet's call to the nations to submit to Babylon and with Jeremiah's decision to remain in Judah under the Babylonian appointee Gedaliah. In Jeremiah's time, it must have seemed an unreal expression of baseless anti-imperial sentiment. Who could face down the Babylonian army that had already defeated the armies of Assyria and Egypt, hitherto the greatest powers of the time? Of course, it may well be a poem written by the later editors of Jeremiah. If it comes from Jeremiah himself, this pronouncement must have astonished a people accustomed to his calls for submission to the Babylonians!

The basic prophecy, "Babylon shall be destroyed" (Jer. 50:2), is filled out by the following series of statements. The striking element is right up front: "There shall arise against her a nation from the north" (50:3). This refers us, the readers, back to the early chapters of Jeremiah where Judah was threatened with destruction from a powerful enemy from the north, an enemy who turned out to be Babylon. Now, Babylon receives a dose of the same medicine, again from an unnamed nation! The empire cannot get away with a murderous foreign policy, even though God used that policy for righteous purposes. The day will come when no inhabitants shall remain to Babylon (50:3). In that day, the people of Israel and the people of Judah together shall return—to seek their God (50:4)! They will not forget the eternal covenant. In verses 6–7, the Holy One reminisces. "My people" are a wandering flock led astray by their shepherds, shepherds being a standard biblical metaphor for kings. In the book of Jeremiah, Judah's kings have tried to maintain independence from the empire, a policy that Jeremiah understands as refusal of God's command. Therefore, "all those who found them devoured them" without feeling guilt, for the kings had forsaken their God and sinned against the Holy One.

The final lines of this prophecy (Jer. 50:8–10) order God's people to flee from Babylon, now that God is "raising up" a new enemy from the north. Babylon will be laid waste, Babylon's plunderers sated with abundance! For a people who lived in the heart of the empire, as did many Judeans after the first deportation of 597 B.C.E., this must have seemed brazenly unpatriotic, disloyal to the nation that had taken them in when their own country was destroyed. Without this final prophecy, however, the work of the prophet Jeremiah and the book that bears his name cannot be understood. The last word of the God of Israel to Babylon is that its day will come! The Babylonians must not allow their many triumphs to render them cocky and invulnerable in their own minds. Nobody will be invulnerable on the day of God's vengeance!

Come, share in the vengeance of the Holy One against Babylon! (Jeremiah 50:11–16). This poem is dominated by the theme of God's vengeance against Babylon for unspecified sin (Jer. 50:14). She will be turned into a desert, the last of nations (50:12), and there will be no normal economic life of planting and reaping (50:16). The idea is to restore justice when the weak have been wronged by the strong—an idea with devastating consequences for an empire, which by its very nature as a military power is involved in oppressive actions against weaker nations.

Formally, the poem is dominated by commands to "you" (plural), presumably addressing the nations. Although these commands appear only in verses 14–15, they seem to pull the whole piece together, calling the oppressed nations to participate in God's destruction of the destroyer. "What she did, do to her!" In contrast to the apostle Paul's advice (Rom. 12:19), vengeance here belongs not only to God, but also to the victims. Their participation serves to restore their dignity and give them a feel for justice. In the end, each nation shall return to its own land (Jer. 50:16), recovering the status it had before the Babylonian invasions. In our days, one thinks of the Palestinians, a nation displaced by the British empire to make room for the Jewish people who burdened European conscience. The successor U.S. empire has continued to support the exclusion of these people from their lands or a vastly reduced form of the proposal of United Nations resolution 242 that is still the position of the international community. This applies both to the Oslo accords, which were never endorsed by the Palestinians, and to the U.S. Roadmap to Peace of 2003. Surely, God's vengeance will mean at least full Palestinian control of a usuable share of the land that was theirs until the British authorities used Jewish refugees to drive them out!

God has forgiven Israel (Jeremiah 50:17–20). This short piece gives a brief refresher on Israel's recent victimization by Assyria and Babylon in turn as the foundation for a "therefore" that promises to punish Babylon as Assyria has already been punished. Israel's sin will no longer be found—not because of conversion, though one supposes that conversion is called for—but because "I will forgive the survivors" (50:20). The application to Palestine seems especially apt!

The day of your visitation has come, Babylon! (Jeremiah 50:21–34). This long poetic section, probably pieced together from several smaller ones, picks up on the idea of God's vengeance and the invitation to join in it, a theme we already found in Jeremiah 50:11–16. Although the vengeance of the Holy One is mentioned explicitly in Jeremiah 50:28, the dominating motif is the "time of their visitation" (50:27) or "the time when I visit them" (50:31). When God "visits" in the Bible, it usually refers to the day when God asks for the accounts of the nations and hands out judgments, as happens in several of Jesus' parables. Again in this poem, we have the call to "do to her all she has done" (v. 29, recalling v. 15).

It is disconcerting to some that Jesus, a preacher of love and forgiveness, puts so great an emphasis on judgment when he envisions the final in-gathering of the world. (This is especially true in the Gospel of Matthew but also in the visions of Revelation.) As peaceable Christians, we would like to have a more developed notion of the joys of our eternal salvation. We do find images of a banquet (Mt. 8:11) and the tree of life, with medicinal leaves and fruit all year long, lining the main boulevard of the city descended from heaven (Rev. 22:1–3), but much less is said about blessedness than about judgment on the wicked. We should probably understand this imbalance in the context of a marginal people like the Jews, subjugated by a mighty Roman empire that had reduced them to poverty and lack of pride as it arrogantly occupied their lands. In such a context, reproduced in many lands today, judgment on the oppressor must be the beginning of salvation.

The final piece of this long poem (Jer. 50:33–34) is directed to Israel. Israel and Judah have been oppressed, and their captors hold on fast and refuse to release them. But *Israel has a redeemer!* The redeemer has taken up Israel's case against Babylon and will hand out rest to the former but unrest to the latter. Again, we see how Babylon's destruction is entailed in the salvation of Israel. Some today speak of a "global village" where we are all related. Mainline economists who have won recent Nobel prizes speak of a "global market." It was true also in the days of Jeremiah that nations affect one another, although the geographical extent of his world was less than that of ours. Then as now, there existed a dominant world power, and its name then was Babylon. When a world is organized this way, there can be no salvation for the dominated nations without a "vengeance" of some sort on the empire that has victimized the rest of the peoples of the world.

To the sword! (Jeremiah 50:35–40). This striking poetic piece celebrates the deeds of "the sword" against Babylon. Five lines begin with the word "sword" in verses 35–37, and verse 38 begins with the similar (in Hebrew) sounding word "drought." The resulting rhythmic pattern can be appreciated even in translation. In Hebrew, the word for sword, *cherev,* begins with a guttural sound that doesn't exist in European languages (except for the Spanish *jota,* which is due to Arabic influence). The sonorous effect of the repetition must have been impressive in a culture where prophecies were heard aloud rather than read silently. The treasures that the sword attacks in Jeremiah 50:37 recall the "treasures" of God's weapons deposit in Jeremiah

30:25. These links between different poems show that this chapter is not a casual miscellany but a planned prophetic "attack" on the empire.

The sword's rampage will leave Babylon without human inhabitants, a refuge for hyenas and other wild animals. The reference to Sodom and Gomorrah reminds us that the sword is executing the judgment of God for exploitation and neglect of the poor (Ezek. 16:49-50).

Babylon's collapse will be an earthquake for the nations (Jeremiah 50:41–46). This prophecy begins with images of military invasion against Babylon. Babylon's morale will collapse in the face of a well-armed invader (Jer. 50:41–43). The mighty army will attack from the north, an allusion to the initial threats against Israel in the book of Jeremiah. But of course, the enemy is only an agent for Israel's Holy One. "Who is like me?" (50:44) God has planned well for Babylon's collapse (50:45). It will be an earthquake for the nations (50:46)!

We might compare this to the unexpected collapse of the Soviet Union in the days of Michail Gorbachov. What a global earthquake! Some nations, like Poland and the small Baltic states, celebrated it as liberation from oppression. Others, like Cuba, the People's Republic of Korea, and Viet Nam, lost a major commercial partner and political support. The U.S. government received it as a victory in the so-called Cold War, the long-term effort to isolate the Soviet Union and surround it with hostile states. In any case, it was an earthquake! So Jeremiah understood the imminent collapse of Babylon.

God avenges and Israel is saved (Jeremiah 51:1–10). This reads like one poem with two parts. In the first half (Jer. 51:1–5), God is the speaker to all hearers, *urbi et orbi* ("to the city and to the world"), and in the second half (51:6–10), God speaks to the people of Israel. In the first, God announces the intention to destroy Babylon. Winnowers will be sent to drive her away in the wind and archers sent to destroy without pity. Verse 5 ties this divine plan to God's intention that Israel not be widowed, thus preparing the second part of the poem.

The second portion is dominated by commands to Israel, beginning with the call to flee from Babylon in order to survive the catastrophe that will be worked by God's vengeance. Verse 7 mentions Babylon's golden cup, which reminds the reader of God's cup of wrath in Jeremiah 25. Here, the cup holds Babylon's wrathful action among the nations, for which she will suffer a sudden fall. (In Hebrew, cities—Jerusalem, Samaria, Babylon—are grammatically feminine, but nations are usually not.) Verses 8b–9a call Israel to administer medicine to stricken Babylon, to which Israel responds that it has done so, but the patient has not been healed.

The poem ends with a glorious quotation in which Israel declares the salvations that the Holy One has wrought on its behalf. It makes a fitting conclusion to a poem that begins with vengeance on the empire and moves into the closely related message of salvation for the oppressed nations, especially Israel. Here, we have the heart of the message of the prophet of this book. God used Babylon for a purpose against all the weak nations of the time, but these actions allowed and intended by God are the occasion for God's vengeance in order to save Israel (and the others).

This calls for some soul-searching for a Christian church that lives in connivance with empire today. If we take the messages of Habakkuk, Nahum, Obadiah, Jeremiah, and John the visionary (to mention only the most vocal prophets of doom against various empires) as the word of God, we must distance ourselves from imperial foreign policy in the nation where we have some influence, the very nation that is today's empire. The biblical prophets unanimously declare that empire provokes God's vengeance, which leads to the collapse of empire. Some prophets, especially Jeremiah, also recognize a legitimate role for empire in God's governance. This should make the message easier to accept for U.S. Christians. There were good intentions behind the imperial policies, first to civilize the lands occupied by nomadic peoples of the woods, the plains, and the mountains of "the West," and then to defend peoples like the Cubans and the Filipinos from oppressive empires. The United States was one of the founders of the United Nations, even though today it usually ignores this community of peoples, apparently considering the other nations as lesser entities who don't understand their own best interests. Although there is much to criticize here, surely God is able to use this military might for some human benefit. God's people may, at times, call as did Jeremiah for submission to this kind of power, but rule by military might will not go unpunished. God's call to flee Babylon seems especially appropriate for Christians living within the United States. For them, such flight begins by withdrawing support for military enterprises that humankind condemns, and supporting instead the struggle to limit and ultimately abolish nuclear weapons and to ban personal land mines. (The current empire, of course, opposes such bans because it wants to reserve the use of these weapons for its own purposes.) God give us strength and wisdom to "flee" this empire and its destructive policies!

Israel confesses a cosmic-historical faith (Jeremiah 51:11–19). This oracle is a statement on the lips of the people of God, in three parts: a survey of God's destruction of Babylon as part of a plan (Jer. 51:11–14), a confessional statement of the creative acts of God (51:15–16), and a contrast between this real God and the false gods of Babylon (51:17–19). The whole is well structured and gives an important confession of faith.

The novel element in the recital of God's intentions to destroy Babylon, a theme well traveled in the book of Jeremiah by now, is the introduction of Media as God's instrument for this purpose (51:11). In fact, Medes and Persians joined to displace the ancient Elamite civilization and conquer Babylon under Cyrus in 539 B.C.E. Our text seems to know this event (indicating that it comes from editors, and not the prophet himself). Again, the coming destruction is termed God's vengeance (51:11). As in previous oracles, we have a call to participate in the sack of Babylon (51:12).

The next two parts of this poem repeat, almost word for word, Jeremiah 10:12–16, the satire on the gods of Babylon and the nations. The confession of the creative deeds of God is in the style of the praise psalms. The treasure-store from which God draws the winds (51:16) reminds us of other treasuries in the oracles concerning the nations (Jer. 48:7; 49:4; 50:25 and 37). The usages of the word "treasure/treasury" are varied. In Jeremiah 48:7 and 49:4, Moab and Ammon are accused of trusting in their treasuries to defend them against the empire. In Jeremiah 50:37, the sword of God will destroy Babylon's treasures. The two other references are to God's treasures—God's weapons in Jeremiah 50:25 and the heavenly storehouse whence come the winds in our present text.

Israel's confession ends by contrasting the Holy One, who is its "portion," with the gods of the nations that are false (*sheqer*). It is a bold statement! Most of the evidence pointed to the power of Bel of Babylon. Babylonian armies conquered and destroyed to the east and to the west, even as far as rich Egypt. The temple of Israel's Holy One, like the temples of the gods of other small and weak nations, lay in ruins. To confess the Holy One in such circumstances as the Maker of everything (Jer. 51:19) must have seemed to many, even many Israelites, as whistling in the dark. It must be similarly hard to be a believer in Palestine today. The God of the United States and of Israel seems to be able to provide wealth and military might, while the God of some Palestinians just calls them to a noble martyrdom in the confidence that ultimate victory will be on their part. Are we to follow the current theory that might makes right, that one can retaliate for a bomb on a bus killing three Israelis with a missile that destroys police headquarters in Palestine and kills dozens of Palestinians? Or, is God partial to the weak and the poor in a world tilted so drastically against them? Israel confesses in the oracle we are reading that the Holy One is the true God and that empire will not prevail against the right of the poor.

God's club (Jeremiah 51:20–24). This striking poem interrupts the general thought of the oracles concerning Babylon to remind the reader that Jeremiah is not just *against* Babylon. Rather, Babylon the empire has played a role that is fully within the plans of the Holy One of Israel. God has many judgments to render on the peoples of the world, and Babylon has been God's club to execute the judgments. This oracle, then, is more in line with the book of Jeremiah through chapter 49 than with the oracles concerning Babylon that make up chapters 50 and 51.

The poem is constructed around one Hebrew verb, *nfts*, "to shatter or break in pieces." The poem opens with a participial form, literally, "*The breaking one,* you (masculine singular) are" (Jer. 51:20). The next six lines begin with a first person singular, "and I will break with you." The effect is to drill the thought into the mind of the listener or reader: God is using a masculine "thou," unnamed until the last verse, to execute judgment. The shatterer is probably Persia or Cyrus the Persian (one would expect a feminine for the city Babylon), but God is going to take vengeance on him in the end for the evil done to Zion! The final you ("your eyes," 51:24) is masculine plural and refers to Israel.

In a way, this little poem summarizes the whole message of the book of Jeremiah. It poses a moral problem for modern Christian readers. Jeremiah never doubts that the military might of empire, Babylon and then Persia, can be and is used for God's purposes. Moab, Edom, Syria, and even Israel can be legitimately destroyed by imperial armies carrying out God's commands. But can imposed military solutions be adequate for any situation? Most Christians, except for certain fringe groups, accept the use of firearms by police forces as a legitimate means of controlling those who violate the peace of their neighbors. Can this also apply to wars, the actions of one nation toward another with military impositions based on greater might? In the twentieth century, there is one war that most Christians feel would meet the moral criteria that justify police actions, the alliance of Communist and capitalist powers against a Nazi Germany that was practicing mass murder. But this was not the war of an empire. One might say it was a league of imperial powers, some in decline and another in ascent, against another aspirant to an empire based on mass murder. Or, one might wish to interpret it as a war of European civilization—capitalist and communist together—and qualify it as a legitimate war, using military power in a morally (and divinely?) approved fashion.

The twentieth century saw many frankly imperial wars, beginning with the Boer War by the British against the Afrikaner farmers in South Africa, and including the U.S. wars against Viet Nam and Iraq, the latter with a thin U.N. veneer. And the second invasion of Iraq, in this twenty-first century, had not even that, only a "coalition of the willing." Frankly, it is hard to see that God could have been using the British or the U.S. armies as a club to punish evildoers, although some Christians believe this to be the case. The book of Jeremiah makes it feasible to make such a case, though, for the well-being of humankind, one would have to examine each case very, very carefully. The poem in Jeremiah 51:20–24 indicates that even when Jeremiah had no doubts that God was using Babylon, the empire was not free from guilt, and its actions would eventually provoke God's vengeance. The use of imperial military might must be seen as wrong until proven otherwise.

Babylon's warriors shall become women (Jeremiah 51:25–33). In this section, we have words of the Holy One announcing destruction to "you" (masculine singular; the Babylonian nation?) in Jeremiah 51:25–26, followed by a call to the nations to make war in Jeremiah 51:27–29, ending with the statement about the Babylonian soldiers becoming women (51:30–32) and the sad fate of the "daughter of Babylon" (51:33). The invitation to the nations to make war in Jeremiah 51:27–29 is one we have already seen. That is how the divine judgment is to be carried out—by human armies. The list of nations in verse 27, however, is a novelty, centered as it is in the Armenian mountains of what is today eastern Turkey. These nations are to join Media (a more expected enemy of Babylon, 51:28) in consecrating war against the tyrants. Poetically, the most interesting images in this section are the soldiers becoming women (51:30) and the daughter of Babylon being a threshing floor to be stomped upon at the time of the harvest (51:33).

Babylon will vomit her choice morsel (Jeremiah 51:34–58). This long piece is complex, made up of several different poems about the fate of Babylon and the related salvation of Israel. It opens with a reference to how Nebuchadnezzar (here, Nebuchadrezzar) king of Babylon devoured Israel and a brief reference to being spewed out (51:34). The same image recurs in quite different language in verse 44. It is the dominant image of the whole piece. The idea of empires devouring the "delicacies" of weaker nations seems an appropriate image for geopolitical realities in the capitalist world of the last five centuries. Father Bartolomé de Las Casas, OP, Bishop of Chiapas, in his *Brevísima relación de la destrucción de las Indias* (1552), blamed the destruction of the New World by European Christians on the Christians' greed (*cobdicia*). Later, in his codicil to the Council of Indies shortly before his death (1562), he appealed to the Council to return the gold and other treasures "stolen" from the Indies for the sake of the salvation of the souls of the Catholic kings and the Spanish nation, which was living in mortal sin because of this massive theft. Capitalist imperialism is based on two economic motives, the search for raw materials in the weaker nations and the search for places to invest idle capital. In recent decades, oil has been the most prized raw material and cheap labor in sweatshops the major source of investment for empires in the colonized parts of the world. But capitalist imperialism began with the colonization of the New World by Spain and Portugal, Christian nations searching for gold and other minerals, for the exploitation of which they used the labor of the native populations. This is the modern form in which the devouring takes place, and it is an analog of the very different economic realities of the Babylonian empire of the sixth century B.C.E.

Jeremiah sends the word of judgment to the capital (Jeremiah 51:59–64). The work of the prophet ends in MT Jeremiah with his orders to Seraiah the scribe to carry out a bold task in Babylon itself. In chapter 36, Jeremiah had written the judgment against Jerusalem in a book that he had Baruch read in the temple to the authorities there. That was in the fourth year of Jehoiakim (605 B.C.E.). Now, Jeremiah writes a book of the judgments against Babylon (the judgments in Jer. 50—51?) and gives it to Seraiah the scribe, apparently a brother to Baruch, to take to Babylon and read there. According to Jeremiah 51:59, Seraiah went with Zedekiah to Babylon in his fourth year (593 B.C.E.). For Seraiah to have accepted this task from the prophet seems incredibly brave, making us lament the lack of more information on this man. Jeremiah gives no instructions on who is to hear the reading of the book of the word of God against Babylon (in contrast to Jer. 36:6, where Jeremiah instructs Baruch to read the first book to the "people of Judah" in the temple at Jerusalem). Only the location is mentioned and not the intended audience. It does not seem possible that such a book could be read to imperial authorities without grave consequences for the king of Judah, Seraiah, and their diplomatic party. So, it seems more likely that the reading was done at an assembly of the exiles in Babylon, the same audience that somewhat later heard Second Isaiah's appeals to get ready to return to Jerusalem. Of course, the authorities would find out what had been read, but it would not be as direct a challenge as if it had been read to the Babylonian leaders. Empires disapprove of those who question their purposes, but they may tolerate such questioning. They do not tolerate open challenges to their hegemony. Thus, hostile resolutions in the U.N. General Assembly may be tolerated, but the appointment of Nora Astorga, who had executed a general who carried out U.S. orders in Managua, as Nicaraguan ambassador to Washington, was rejected by the Reagan administration, which perceived it as a direct challenge to its control of the region.

"Thus far are the words of Jeremiah." The end. It is finished.

PART A'

Prose Conclusion:
The Fall of Jerusalem
(Jeremiah 52)

The last chapter of the book of Jeremiah is about the fall of Jerusalem. It is all narrative material, with nothing that claims to be from the prophet Jeremiah, whose prophecies conclude with the oracles against Babylon in chapters 50—51. The historical content of chapter 52 is for the most part not new. Almost all of Jeremiah 52 is a word for word repetition of large portions of 2 Kings 24:18—25:30. Some of its material related to the fall of Jerusalem has already appeared in Jeremiah 39—40. Why then did the editors of this book include this narrative material, which does not even mention Jeremiah? The answer is probably the same as it was for Jeremiah 39:1–10, another passage narrating the fall of Jerusalem without mentioning the prophet. In both cases, the narrative shows that the word of God spoken by Jeremiah was carried out by the Babylonians.

In terms of the structure of the book, Jeremiah 52 corresponds to the historical introduction in Jeremiah 1:1–3. There, Jeremiah was introduced by placing him in the context of the Davidic kings who presided over the last decades of the kingdom of Judah. The ring structure of MT Jeremiah required some sort of correspondence, and the result is a historical frame made up of Jeremiah 1:1–3 and 52:1–34. Where the introduction gave a broad chronological frame for Jeremiah's ministry, the conclusion limits itself to the fall of Jerusalem, the working out of the word that Jeremiah delivered during his long ministry.

The Holy One Punishes Zedekiah (Jeremiah 52:1–3)

The core of this little paragraph is the affirmation that Zedekiah "did what was evil in the eyes of the Holy One, just as Jehoiakim had done." It is the familiar summary that the authors of the books of Kings offer concerning each king; this one can be found in 2 Kings 24:19. Zedekiah was a son of Hamutal, daughter of Jeremiah of Libnah, and this Hamutal was also the mother of Jehoahaz, the first son of Josiah, according to 2 Kings 23:31. In other words, Zedekiah was a son of Josiah, the "good" king according to the books of Kings. The readers of Jeremiah know him as a king who wanted to hear the word of God (see Jer. 21:1–2; 37:17), who was willing to protect Jeremiah from his worst enemies (Jer. 37:21; 38:7–13), but who rejected God's orders to submit to the king of Babylon in order to save his life. For readers of the book, this is the evil of Zedekiah. All of the evils that befell Jerusalem during his reign are the outworkings of that refusal, exactly as Jeremiah had threatened (Jer. 21:1–10; 38:17–23). Thus, even though Jeremiah 52 does not mention Jeremiah or the word of God, the reader is expected to understand the connection.

The Disgraceful End of Zedekiah and the Ruin of Jerusalem (Jeremiah 52:4–27)

In one paragraph (52:4–11), the fate of Zedekiah is expounded: his sons killed before his eyes, and then he himself blinded and taken captive to Babylon. Neither God nor Jeremiah are mentioned, in a fashion very similar to the narration in Jeremiah 39:1–10. This is not a secular version of history nor the methodologically distant stance of the academic historian. God's hand does not have to be visible for the trained reader to discern it, and, by this point in the book, the repeated message of Jeremiah will have trained the reader.

A second paragraph (Jer. 52:12–16) tells of the burning of the city and the deportation of its population. The temple and every big house were burned down, and the walls of the city were destroyed. But when exile is mentioned in verses 15–16, there is a remarkable observation: Nebuzaradan, the officer in charge of the destruction, makes a distinction among the population. He takes into exile a portion of the people, among which the artisans are pointed out, but he leaves behind the poorest people of the land to be vinedressers and tillers of the soil! In the economy of Judah, these peasants were the productive sector, and evidently Babylon wished to have a going concern in this province. These verses are not present in LXX Jeremiah, which almost surely means they were added (from 2 Kings 25:11–12) in the final revision of the book. If we remember that this revision was done by the scribes of the Babylonian exile, whose hostility to Zedekiah and his followers as well as toward the Egyptian exile community is evident earlier in the book of Jeremiah, we should probably recognize a certain self-criticism here. They, the legitimate heirs of the Davidic promises, were not the bulk of the people of Judah nor were they the ones who made the economy work. Alternatively, they may simply have believed that the only people who count are city dwellers, who make history and suffer its consequences. The ordinary people, the vast majority, survive under all regimes and pose no threat to any regime.

In our time, the most dynamic economic sector is the financial one where fortunes are made by exchanges that produce nothing. This is the "casino economy," where one's win is another's loss because no new fortunes are produced by making goods. In those sectors that do not just exchange values from one hand to another, the driving forces with the largest investments are for production related to the military, producing goods that are designed to destroy and be destroyed in the process. A strange empire this one! It stands to reason that when this empire collapses, it will be the military and financial sectors that will fall hardest. Like the peasants of Jeremiah's time, the producers of milk, shoes, houses, and other productive goods will probably be able to survive more readily than the dealers in stocks and in weapons.

The next paragraph (Jer. 52:17–27) deals with the fate of the religious establishment of Jerusalem. The metal implements and pillars of the temple were sacked, apparently melted down by the Babylonians so that the metals could be put to other uses. The priests in charge of the worship of the Holy One were taken to the king of Babylon at Riblah and executed there on his orders. Thus, the religious establishment ordained by God at Sinai and implemented according to the books of Moses was destroyed because it assisted the Davidic kings in proclaiming a faith that emphasized God's protective presence without also demanding obedience to God's demands for justice, at least according to this paragraph in the context of Jeremiah's prophecies. One can hardly expect the religion of the state to survive the destruction of that state, even if that religion is theologically "true."

The Statistics of the Babylonian Exile (Jeremiah 52:28–30)

"So Judah went into exile out of its land" (Jer. 52:27b). Our text, with some unadorned demographic statistics, tells what that in fact meant. The whole passage, beginning with verse 27b, is absent from the LXX and is evidently an addition, like the distinction among Judahites at the moment of the invasion that is mentioned in verses 15–16. The statistics reveal an unexpected picture of the Babylonian exile, an event that transformed the life of the Israelites and laid the basis for Second Temple Judaism. The largest group, 3,023 persons, went with Jehoiachin in 598 B.C.E. Only 832 persons were taken with Zedekiah in 586 B.C.E., and then 745 persons five years later, probably when Gedaliah was murdered—a total of only 4600 persons in the exilic community! It is difficult to reach a good calculation of the total population of Judah at the time, but a conservative figure would put it at 250,000. This means that the great Babylonian exile that led to the writing of most of the books of the Bible was made up of a small percentage of the population of Judah!

Why do the editors of Jeremiah give us these statistics? We presume that, for them, these 4600 persons are the people who really count. In any nation, the makers of history are a relatively small sector of the population, but that fact is seldom as openly recognized as it is here. Here, we have an admission of the weakness of a restoration project that did not include the poorest people of Judah, who were both the majority and the producers of food for all Judeans. There is an element of self-criticism here, a self-criticism in line with the biblical idea that God is a God of the poor and the excluded, as we see it depicted in Luke's "Christmas" story of the birth of Jesus in a stable among animals, an outcast among his people.

Hope for the Davidic Line (Jeremiah 52:31–34)

The book of Jeremiah takes for its ending the final paragraph of the books of Kings (2 Kings 25:27–30), which describes the release of Jehoiachin from confinement in Babylon. This happened in the thirty-seventh year of his "reign," which was also the thirty-seventh year of his confinement, the year 562 B.C.E. in the chronological system we use today. The reader is reminded of Jeremiah 24, where the Babylonian exiles were good figs when compared to King Zedekiah and those who remained in Jerusalem with him, the bad figs. She is also reminded of the hope-filled promises of Jeremiah 30—33, chapters that include specific promises to the Davidic line (Jer. 33:14–26, an addition of MT Jeremiah lacking in LXX Jeremiah). The release of Jehoiachin is read in the book of Jeremiah, as also in Kings, as an anticipation of that hope and promise for the Davidites.

And so, Jeremiah ends with hope for the future of Israel, not just for the people but for the political organization of its state. Babylon, the empire, does not have the last word, although Nebuchadnezzar was a servant of the Holy One of Israel to execute God's plan of "visitation" on Jerusalem and the nations of its world. For Christians, the last word is God's action in raising Jesus, one of the many victims of imperial "justice," from the dead. As with the release of Jehoiachin, the resurrection is not yet the kingdom of God announced by Jesus to his listeners in Galilee, but it is a sign that the promise is still in place and hope is in order. As Babylon was used by God and then in due time visited by the same God for judgment, we must also hope that the U.S. empire will one day be "visited" and that we or our children will be able to move toward the kingdom where the greatest is the one who serves the most (Mk. 10:41–45). Christians who happen also to be U.S. citizens need not feel sad about the prospect of the collapse of the U.S. empire. To make a community of nations where each has a say in what happens, a true United Nations where all are respected, can only be a gain for all nations, freeing U.S. citizens of the burden of the bloated military and police forces that are needed to protect them in a world where they are the oppressors of the weak.

Of course, the U.S. empire is built on a "free market" dominated by enterprises based in the U.S. and other wealthy nations, and a postimperial world will require a different kind of economy with much more local control over the production and distribution of goods. This will no doubt require a long period of adjustments that will, for those accustomed to wild consumption, be perceived as a loss of standard of living. In terms of human satisfactions, this need not be really so. When we can restore a world in which wealth is measured by human satisfactions and by the creation of community, we can live in greater security and peace among neighbors. That security and peace will be gains greatly surpassing the loss of some gadgets that add little to the quality of the lives we live. This is hardly the place to try to spell out the specifics. We must be willing to affirm with conviction our faith in the passion and resurrection of Christ Jesus as the way into a human future for our world. This means, at a minimum, willingness to accept the death of empire to allow God to raise our world to a new and fuller life. Such a life is announced in the resurrection of Jesus Christ, as it was in the book of Jeremiah by the release of Jehoiachin from prison.

Glory to God in the highest and peace on earth!

Bibliography

Brueggemann, Walter. *A Commentary on Jeremiah: Exile & Homecoming.* Grand Rapids: Eerdmans, 1998. This is an excellent commentary, much along the lines of "Commentaries for Today," except longer. It has a bit more technical usage but is quite accessible.

Nicholson, Ernest W. *Preaching to the Exiles: A Study of the Prose Tradition in the Book of Jeremiah.* Oxford: Blackwell, 1970. A fine study of the material defined in the title; not technical.

Overholt, Thomas W. *The Threat of Falsehood: A Study in the Theology of the Book of Jeremiah.* Naperville: Allenson, 1970. A good study of a major theme of the book of Jeremiah.

Welch, Adam C. *Jeremiah: His Time and His Work.* Oxford: 1951 reprint of a 1928 original. Old but good.

Revista de Interpretación Bíblica Latinoamericana (Journal of Latin American Biblical Interpretation) 35–36 (2000). This issue of *RIBLA* is devoted to "Los libros proféticos: La voz de los profetas y sus relecturas," with articles on Jeremiah by Jorge Torreblanca, Alicia Winters, J. Severino Croatto, and Jorge Pixley. It can be ordered by e-mail at lauren@uio.satnet.net, or by fax (an international call from the United States to Ecuador) at 011-593-2-566150.

Notes

Introduction

[1]The Masoretic Text is the Hebrew of the great medieval biblical manuscripts based on scholarship of first millennium Jewish textual experts, the Masoretes. Printed Bibles are based on a manuscript preserved in a museum at Leningrad/St. Petersburg.

[2]B.C.E. stands for "Before Common Era" and C.E. stands for "Common Era." These abbreviations replace B.C. and A.D. in archaeological dating in order to distinguish historical judgments from Christian faith statements.

[3]Jorge Torreblanca, *Jeremías, T.M. Una búsqueda de estructuración global del texto canónico*, doctoral dissertation at ISEDET, the major Protestant theological school in Buenos Aires, 1990, under the direction of Jose Severino Croatto.

[4]This translation was done by Jews in Alexandria in the third century B.C.E. Legend has it that the translators were seventy wise men, hence the symbol LXX.

Part A: Prose Introduction

[1]The issue of the name of God is a difficult one. The Hebrew Bible gives the God of Israel a name with the consonants YHWH. But it caused discomfort in Israel to call God by the name. The LXX in the third century B.C.E. eliminated the name, using *kyrios* (Greek for "Lord") in its place. When vowel points were added to the Hebrew Bible a few centuries later, the vowels for *adonai* (Hebrew for "Lord") were written with the consonants YHWH to serve as a reminder that what the reader should say aloud was *adonai*, not YHWH.

What are we to do when we read the Bible today? In this commentary, I will use "the Holy One" where the MT has YHWH. This is a way to avoid lightly mouthing the Name whose holiness is inexpressible. It has the disadvantage of failing to recognize the particularity of a God who does have a name. A name that cannot be said seems right for God, who is singular like a person who has his or her own name, but who is also unique in virtue of being capable of identification without a name as the *only* Creator of all else and hence definable by nature without requiring a name to designate "him" (on gender, see the next note).

Part B: Prophet to the Nations

[1]The Bible refers to the Holy One in masculine terms. The Bible does mention female divinities, most prominently Asherah, who was worshiped in the Jerusalem temple alongside the Holy One (1 Kings 15:13; 2 Kings 21:7; 23:6; Jer. 44:24–25, queen of heaven, unnamed, either Asherah or Astarte). But in a process associated especially with King Josiah (2 Kings 23), worship came to be limited to just one God, the Holy One (YHWH). The oneness of God is, in fact, basic for later biblical religion and became Judaism's confession of faith in the words of Deut. 6:4. To be able to imagine God as a person, God must be either male or female, since that is how persons exist. When the remaining one God was a male God, female characteristics such as childbirth came to be attributed to him (Deut. 32:18; Ps. 90:2; Isa. 42:14; 46:3; 66:13). These do not make God female, but are female functions of a male God.

This outcome creates an identity and self-esteem problem for the female half of humanity and is therefore unacceptable. Sallie McFague in *Models of God* (Minneapolis: Fortress Press, 1987) has explored female metaphors for God (Mother, Lover, Friend), and this helps us to understand the problem, though it does not resolve our prayer and liturgical difficulties with gendered God-language. In this commentary, I will try to avoid gendered language for God, although I recognize that the God of Israel is referred to as male in the Bible. It is imperative that we search for a new language, although at this stage it entails a certain awkwardness ("God Godself," "God and God's people," and so forth).

Part C: Judah's Sentence

[1]The term *Deuteronomistic* is used by biblical scholars to refer to literature inspired by the book of Deuteronomy, especially the "Deuteronomistic History" contained in Joshua, Judges, and the books of Samuel and Kings. It is clear that some Deuteronomists had a hand in reworking the Jeremiah traditions that have reached us.

Part E: Covenant Suspended

[1]This observation comes from J. N. M. Wijngaards, "HOSI' and HE'ELAH: A Twofold Approach to the Exodus," *Vetus Testamentum* 15 (1965): 91–102.

[2]See Abraham J. Heschel, *The Prophets* (New York: Harper, 1962).

Part F': Conflicts with Kings, Prophets, and Exiles

[1]This expression is attributed to Margaret Thatcher, prime minister of Great Britain in the 1980s, and certainly she believed it whether or not she created the expression. The acronym TINA has entered general economic commentary.